Our American Cousin

Tom Taylor's Comedy Classic

in a New Version

by

LOWELL SWORTZELL

AF278402

Dramatic Publishing Company
Woodstock, Illinois ● Australia ● New Zealand ● South Africa

IMPORTANT BILLING AND CREDIT REQUIREMENTS

All producers of the play *must* give credit to the author of the play in all programs distributed in connection with performances of the play and in all instances in which the title of the play appears for purposes of advertising, publicizing or otherwise exploiting the play and/or a production. The name of the author *must* also appear on a separate line, on which no other name appears, immediately following the title, and *must* appear in size of type not less than fifty percent (50%) the size of the title type. Biographical information on the author, if included in the playbook, may be used in all programs. *In all programs this notice must appear:*

"Produced by special arrangement with
THE DRAMATIC PUBLISHING COMPANY, INC., of Woodstock, Illinois."

This new version of *Our American Cousin* was first presented by Tufts University at the Tufts Arena Theatre, with the following cast:

The Nightwatchman	Dana C. Bate
Peanuts John	Howard Weiner
Florence Trenchard (Laura Keene)	Carol E. Ganem
Abel Murcott	Marvin I. Terban
Asa Trenchard	Thomas Divoll
Sir Edward Trenchard	Maurice Breslow
Mr. Coyle	Dana C. Bate
Lt. Vernon (The Prompter)	William B. Allen
Mr. Binny	John R. Mclean
Buddicombe	John Defelice
John Wickens	Tom Tobin
Lord Dundreary (Mr. Emerson)	Seabury Quinn, Jr.
Mary Meredith	Joyce G. Katz
Mrs. Mountchessington	June Judson
Augusta	Wendy Farer
Georgina	Clare Melley
Skillet	Anne Gordon
A Soldier	Alan Rinzler

Directed by Nancy Foell Swortzell
Settings by Stephen Palestrant
Costumes by Lois Aden

A NOTE ABOUT THE PLAY

Tom Taylor's Adelphi producers rejected *Our American Cousin* in 1851, not foreseeing that it would become the most popular comedy on the 19th Century American stage, and one day even triumph in London for four hundred nights. Laura Keene, the noted American actress-manager, while slightly more impressed, only bought the play because the role of Asa Trenchard well suited a promising young actor in her company named Joseph Jefferson. Even so, the script still might never have been produced if carpenters working on a revival of *Midsummer Night's Dream* had not delayed its opening two weeks, causing Miss Keene to hurry *Our American Cousin* into production as a substitute. Jefferson scored his predicted success along with E. A. Sothern in the ever expanding role of Lord Dundreary. But no one could have predicted the long-lasting popularity of the play itself which opened in New York, October 15, 1858. It was last produced professionally at the Booth Theatre in New York in 1915.

The new version depicts with historical and theatrical accuracy the performance given by Laura Keene and her company in Ford's Theatre, Washington, D.C., the night President Lincoln was assassinated. Of enormous assistance in preparation of this play was the Prompter's Copy of Taylor's script, in The New York Public Library Theatre Collection, written in longhand, giving stage directions—many of which are employed here—and valuable information about the original production. Taylor's comedy survives in three different texts, which have been shortened and unified in this version.

Our American Cousin

A Comedy in Two Acts
For 12m., 6w., extras

CHARACTERS

THE NIGHTWATCHMAN

PEANUTS JOHN, the Stage Doorman

PROMPTER (also plays LT. VERNON)

LAURA KEENE (also plays FLORENCE TRENCHARD)

MR. EMERSON (also plays LORD DUNDREARY)

SKILLET	GEORGINA
BUDDICOMBE	ASA TRENCHARD
MR. BINNY	MR. COYLE
JOHN WICKENS	ABEL MURCOTT
SIR EDWARD TRENCHARD	MARY MEREDITH
MRS. MOUNTCHESSINGTON	A SOLDIER
AUGUSTA	

Also stagehands, property men, servants, etc.

SYNOPSIS

The play takes place on the stage of Ford's Theatre, Washington, D.C., first in the 1890's, then on April 14, 1865, and again in the 1890's.

ACT I: The morning rehearsal.
ACT II: The evening performance.

CHARACTER & COSTUME NOTES

THE NIGHTWATCHMAN: He is a garrulous old man, partially bent over from age, who speaks clearly in a warm and friendly manner, never waiting for answers to his questions or comments upon his remarks. He has a deep sense of the historical significance of the events he describes, as well as an emotional response to the tragedy he nightly relives. He wears an old sweater and jacket, dark trousers and a cap that comes down over his ears to reveal tufts of white hair and whiskers that frame his wrinkled face.

PEANUTS JOHN: Peanuts, a young boy, is something of a simpleton, ever ready to please anyone willing to reward him with a nickel to buy a bag of peanuts. He wears impoverished clothes and possesses unkempt hair, which add to his pitiable state.

FLORENCE TRENCHARD & LAURA KEENE: Florence, a spoiled but well-meaning girl, knows very little about the practical side of life although she is willing to learn. Her sweet beauty and pleasant manner make her extremely attractive. Laura Keene is Florence's opposite because as manager of her own company she is practical, efficient and firm. Her authority is felt by everyone, yet everyone respects her. In the first act she wears a rehearsal dress that reflects Miss Keene's good taste. In the second act she is dressed in Florence's most extravagant gown, every frill of which indicates that she is the leading lady.

ABEL MURCOTT: Murcott, the alcoholic clerk, wears an everyday business suit. His collar is open and his nose is red.

ASA TRENCHARD: Asa, the lean, American clown, is a lovable rustic who charms everyone with his warm folk qualities. Under his rough exterior are a generous heart and Yankee ingenuity. His buckskin clothes resemble those of the typical American pioneer; for his archery outfit he adds an Indian blanket and a feathered headdress. He speaks with a New England twang.

SIR EDWARD TRENCHARD: Sir Edward, a stuffy aristocrat, is easily duped because of his pomposity. He wears the very best suit of the day, realizing too late that he cannot afford it.

MR. COYLE: Coyle, the attorney, is the epitome of nineteenth century melodramatic villains. Sneering and leering, he wears a long black cape, and exudes evil to the extent of prompting the audience to hiss at him. Under the cape he wears a black suit.

LT. VERNON: Vernon, a handsome young man in love with Florence, wears a naval uniform. As the Prompter, he may remove the jacket or coat. As the Prompter, he acts like a well organized stage manager, which, in effect, he must be since he supervises all scene shifts.

MR. BINNY: He is the butler and wears a very stiff uniform which puffs his chest out so it appears about to explode. Because of this he seems to strut rather than walk.

BUDDICOMBE: He is another overly proper servant but less ostentatious in dress and manner than Mr. Binny.

JOHN WICKENS: He is the gardener, a man of simple tastes, who worships Mary. He wears knickers and a farmer's shirt.

SOLDIER: The soldier is a private in the Union Army.

LORD DUNDREARY & MR. EMERSON: Lord Dundreary, one of the great comic eccentrics of our stage, is famous for his dyed red whiskers. Even though a portrait of an imbecile aristocrat at his most inane, he is entirely charming. His clothes are as outlandish as his personality; his second-act suit is garish, a mixture of plaids and stripes in ridiculous color combinations. He wears a monocle, which he uses as a prop. Appropriately,

Mr. Emerson, too, wears a somewhat outlandish suit upon his entrance; to this he may add a different hat, coat or tie after the rehearsal commences.

MARY MEREDITH: Mary is a sweet child of great beauty and simple taste. She is a child of nature who delights in listening to the birds sing and in caring for her dairy. She is dressed in a milkmaid's costume with apron and bonnet.

MRS. MOUNTCHESSINGTON: She is an overbearing woman in her middle years, affected and pompous, and well dressed.

AUGUSTA: She is Mrs. Mountchessington's daughter, who, like her mother, is none too intelligent. She is pretty but always self-conscious of her appearance and dependent upon the advice of her mother in all matters. She is dressed far beyond her means.

GEORGINA: Georgina, the perpetually sick girl, claims to be too delicate to walk or even eat. Yet she constantly sneaks food at every opportunity and is, consequently, greatly overweight. Therefore, her dress, designed for an ethereal creature at death's door, does not suit her.

SKILLET: She is a household servant who wears a Victorian cook's costume. She is, of course, very proper.

PRODUCTION NOTES

THE BASIC SETTING: Only one basic setting is required for this play: the stage of Ford's Theatre in April, 1865. In the beginning the stage is bare except for a few elements of scenery seen at the sides and in the background. The stage should not be visible to any extent during the scenes in which the Night watchman appears; instead, the light should be concentrated on the face of the man himself.

As the stage comes to life during the Nightwatchman's description, old-fashioned footlights begin to burn, and a few pieces of scenery suggesting a wing and border arrangement common to nineteenth century theatres are put in place. Drawings and photographs of Ford's Theatre appear in many books on Lincoln and will prove helpful to the director and designer in arranging their setting. However, there is no need to reproduce the actual theatre since a mere suggestion will be most effective. The play has been presented quite successfully in an arena production with almost no scenery whatever.

On one side of the stage, near the proscenium arch, is the Presidential box. It must contain a light and a chair inside, and be accessible for convenient entrances and exits by the Nightwatchman. During the intermission this box is decorated with American flags and a portrait of George Washington.

PROPERTIES & SCENE SHIFTS: As indicated in the text, the furniture and properties are moved in full view of the audience, as part of the planned action of the play. The director must assign each actor a specific task for each scene shift; these must be performed quickly and quietly, without interrupting the continuity of the play.

Before the play begins, the Prompter's table and stool are put in place, along with several rehearsal chairs for the actors in the first scene. The Prompter carries an oversize copy of the play, which is handwritten, as well as a pencil and various checklists. It should be the responsibility of the Prompter to supervise the shifts as well as to see that each shift is complete before the following scene begins.

The Nightwatchman carries a lantern which gives a dim light. The Drawing Room at Trenchard Manor includes a colorful rug on the floor, one long or round dining table and three Victorian chairs, a side chair, a small love seat, a hanging mirror, an old-fashioned chandelier, two or more potted palms or large house plants, and a French door. The director may use less furniture if he desires. The furniture need not be realistic but should reflect the period of the 1860's in bright colors and reveal a gay, comic spirit. Silverware and china are placed on the table which is covered with a colorful cloth. Also needed are a tea wagon with glasses, a tray with various decanters, a mail pouch with letters, Asa's traveling bags, and a knitting basket with yarn.

The Library at Trenchard Manor is composed of a desk containing a globe, an ink stand, a quill pen, a large family Bible, and a small tray with decanters. Murcott carries a bag with letters and legal documents. A chair stands in back of the desk.

Asa's Room requires a large shower bath containing a small amount of water which spills on Asa's head when he pulls the shower rope. Near the bath stands a bureau with a wash basin, pitcher, and hand towel on top. A small bottle of hair dye is in the top drawer of this bureau. Asa's valises are on the floor, which may have a small rug if desired. A chair stands by a small dressing table.

The Dairy scene consists of a section of picket fence, a rustic wooden bench, a large birdhouse on the end of a long pole, a butter churn, two small stools, rose bower (can be simply several flower pots with flowers in bloom), a large spinning wheel, and a small chair.

The Wine Cellar is suggested by a few painted stones and barrels. One open barrel must be large enough for an actor to fall into. Various bottles of wine and candles stand on a table which is really just another barrel with a board on top of it. A small stool stands in front of this improvised table. The scene is completed with several wooden boxes or wine kegs.

In the picnic scene, large outing blankets and baskets of food and drink are added to the Dairy setting.

The same pieces of furniture and properties may be used in several different scenes in order to simplify the production. For instance, the chairs needed in the Drawing Room may be the same ones used in the Library and in Asa's Room, just as the stools from the Dairy scene may be employed in the Wine Cellar scene.

PROPERTIES

Ford's Theatre: Prompter's table and stool, several straight chairs, pieces of scenery, footlights, presidental box at one side of stage (light and chair in box, also American flags and portrait of Washington to be added later).

Drawing Room, Trenchard Manor: Dining table, three chairs, side chair, love seat, hanging mirror, chandelier, potted palms, rug, French door. Offstage: Luncheon table (for Mr. Binny) with tablecloth, silverware and china; tray of decanters, several glasses, mixers, bowl of sugar (for servants).

Library, Trenchard Manor: Desk and chair; globe, inkstand, quill pen, Bible, small tray with decanters, all on desk.

Asa's Room: Shower bath; bureau; wash basin, pitcher, and hand towel on bureau; bottle of hair dye in top drawer of bureau; dressing table, chair, small rug, Asa's valises.

Dairy Scene: Section of picket fence, rustic wooden bench, large birdhouse on pole, butter churn, two small stools, several potted flowers, spinning wheel, chair.

Wine Cellar: Large open barrel, table made of barrel and board, candles and bottles of wine on "table," stool, various boxes or kegs, case with paper in it.

Picnic Scene: Blankets, baskets of food and drink, added to Dairy setting.

Nightwatchman: Lantern.

Peanuts John: Bag of peanuts (in the shell).

Prompter: Copy of play, pencil, checklists, coin in pocket, list of properties, cigar in pocket, matches.

Buddicombe: Newspaper (Act I), tray and glasses, corked bottle (Act II).

Skillet: Dustcloth or feather duster.

John Wickens: Mail pouch containing a number of letters, two milk pails on a yoke, spinning wheel.

Dundreary: Handkerchief, monocle.

Georgina: Fan.

Asa Trenchard: Valise, letter, paper in pocket (Act I); two milk pails on a yoke, bottle of hair dye (same as used in Act I), whittling knife and stick, cigar and match, will in pocket (Act II).

Mr. Binny: Bunch of mint, several straws.

Mr. Murcott: Bag containing various papers, including legal document with seals on it.

Augusta: Bow (for Mrs. Mountchessington).

Florence: Paper.

Mr. Coyle: Keys in pocket, key on watch chain (Act II).

Sir Edward: Pistol (Act II).

Note: See Production Notes for fuller descriptions of property items.

Our American Cousin

ACT I

SCENE: *Ford's Theatre, Washington, D.C., in the 1890's.*

AT RISE OF CURTAIN: *The play begins on a totally dark stage. After a moment footsteps are heard, then the sound of a door opening. Lantern light spills on stage from the open doorway where the silhouetted figure of the NIGHT· WATCHMAN appears. He raises and lowers the lantern in an effort to determine the identity of the intruder.*

NIGHTWATCHMAN. Ain't no one allowed trespassing. *(There is no answer.)* I said you're breaking the law coming in here. *(Still there is no reply.)* This is Federal property, you know. What you want this time of night, anyway? There's nothing here for thieves, you can be certain of that. Nothing but memories. Lord knows, you're welcome to take away as many of them as you like. Where you think you're going now in those shadows? Careful where you walk. The floor won't hold up in some places, and there's wreckage all about us. That's why I keep folks out. The Government don't want anything else to happen. And the way I look on it, there's been trouble enough in this building already to last till the end of time, Lord knows. *(Looking down.)* Loose timbers fallen from upstairs. Now if you insist on poking about, you better let me show you the way around. I ain't suppose' to. But it appears I can't stop you lurking in the dark. Besides, this time of night, no one will suspect one way or another. And I don't care what they tell you, there ain't a watchman on Earth but what's glad for somebody to talk the night out with—especially in a crumbling tomb like this. Hard to believe this was a theater, ain't it? The stage was here. Right over here. Come along, I'll show you. There was boxes on the sides of the stage like they used to do in those days. *(When he indicates the boxes with his lantern, they come dimly into view.)* And the scenery was right about here. *(As the stage lights come up, a piece of Victorian scenery glides down into place behind the NIGHTWATCH-MAN.)* Down there were the footlights. Gas, they used then … glowed a yellow glow, I remember. *(The footlights come on.)* And back this way was the dressing rooms. That's the stage door there. Peanuts John always stood there.

(PEANUTS JOHN, a young man, something of a simpleton, appears in the doorway, shelling and munching peanuts.)

NIGHTWATCHMAN *(cont'd)*. He took care of the horses out back; stables all along the alley out there. *(Moves to a desk and chair.)* See this: where the Prompter sat.

(The PROMPTER enters and takes his seat.)

NIGHTWATCHMAN *(cont'd)*. Ran the whole show, the Prompter. Of course, when Miss Keene was here she ran everything, including the Prompter. She was a real businesswoman; made more money than any man manager in her day, they say. Musta had a fine head on her shoulders. She had rehearsals here every day because she put on a different play every day.

(The stage of Ford's Theatre, as it was the morning of April 14, 1865, is now fully lighted. Members of the company come on in their street clothes. Some check their lines with the PROMPTER. Others talk softly as they wait in the wings. The NIGHTWATCHMAN has disappeared. Stage-hands, assisted by members of the acting company, place the furniture for the first scene of the rehearsal. PEANUTS JOHN leaves the door and runs to the PROMPTER.)

PEANUTS JOHN. Miss Keene just turned the alleyway.

PROMPTER *(calling out)*. Is everyone ready for rehearsal to begin? Where's Mr. Emerson?

PEANUTS JOHN. Ain't come in yet.

PROMPTER. You better get him from the tavern next door before Miss Keene misses him.

PEANUTS JOHN. I'll get him here. I'll tell him he's late. I'll get him for you. *(Stands perfectly still in front of PROMPT-ER.)* I'll go get him.

PROMPTER. Oh, very well. *(Reaching into his pockets.)* Here's a nickel for peanuts. Now, bring him in here.

PEANUTS JOHN *(smiling)*. I'll tell him. I'll tell him he's late.

(LAURA KEENE enters. A tall, stately woman, she hurries on stage only to confront PEANUTS JOHN on his way out. As soon as she appears, the entire company stops talking and moving scenery, and assembles on stage.)

LAURA KEENE. You're the doorman?

PEANUTS JOHN. Yes, ma'am, Miss Keene.

LAURA KEENE. Then you should be at the door. Isn't that where Mr. Ford expects you to be?

PEANUTS JOHN. I was at the door, Miss Keene. I was. I been standing there all morning. But Mr. Prompter called me away. He called me away, Miss Keene. He said, "Go find Mr. Emerson in a hurry." He gave me money, Miss Keene. He paid me to leave the door. I didn't want to.

LAURA KEENE. If he paid you, then you'd best find Mr. Emerson and earn your money.

PEANUTS JOHN. I'll get him, I will.

LAURA KEENE *(to the company)*. Does anyone know where Mr. Emerson may be located this morning?

PROMPTER. He went to Good Friday services on G Street, I believe I heard him say, Miss Keene.

PEANUTS JOHN. But you told me to look next door.

LAURA KEENE. Then fetch him over, please, from the "church" next door.

PEANUTS JOHN. I'll have him here in a minute, Miss Keene. You can trust me. *(Hurries off.)*

LAURA KEENE *(addressing the company in a businesslike but kind manner)*. About our leaving Washington: The coming weekend may prove difficult, with troops moving and the railways being used by both armies. Then the celebrations of people rejoicing in the streets and attending "Good Friday" services in every tavern across the country have paralyzed movement in the cities. Therefore, we must depart early and be prepared for delays, for which I can only ask your indulgence. Our scenic effects will be ready to leave Mr. Ford's an hour after the performance tonight, and we must have our costumes and personal belongings ready, too. I have hired two wagons to call at midnight, and whatever you do not send then, you will have to carry with you on the train. This is the most satisfactory arrangement I can manage. Surely you understand that with the war over only a week, it is impossible for me to accommodate you as I would like.

(PEANUTS JOHN returns, running up to LAURA KEENE, interrupting her.)

PEANUTS JOHN. He's coming. I got him, Miss Keene. I told you he was next door.

(MR. EMERSON enters and stands in the doorway.)

MR. EMERSON. Happy Good Friday, everybody!

LAURA KEENE *(staring intently)*. Mr. Emerson, the first item on our rehearsal agenda today is your walk. You still do not perform it the way I suggested.

MR. EMERSON. Like this? *(Attempts to hop, but stumbles and falls down awkwardly, the company is unable to refrain from laughing at him.)*

LAURA KEENE. The Dundreary walk, Mr. Emerson, is a little hop. Like this. *(Performs it.)* It's very simple. We'll all do it with you. *(The entire company demonstrates the hop to EMERSON, still sprawled on the stage. He finds the lesson funny and begins to laugh, then gets up and hops about with complete abandon. When the cast begins to laugh, he stops abruptly, and stands embarrassed.)* There, Mr. Emerson, you have it. I knew you could do it. *(To PROMPTER.)* Now we are ready for the rehearsal to begin! With the Capital jubilant, we may expect an unusually good benefit this evening.

PEANUTS JOHN. Grover's Theatre announced a victory celebration for tonight. "Aladdin and His Lamp" with special lights and effects. Young Mr. Ford said everybody is going there.

LAURA KEENE. I hardly think we are going to Grover's, however special the effects!

PEANUTS JOHN. Everybody's already seen "Our American Cousin," it's been playing so long.

LAURA KEENE. But even after a thousand performances they still come.

PEANUTS JOHN. Not tonight. They're going to Grover's. Young Mr. Ford said so.

LAURA KEENE *(to the PROMPTER, in an effort to ignore PEANUTS JOHN)*. We'll begin, please! Everyone in place for the opening scene. *(The actors disperse, some taking places on stage, others retiring to the wings.)* Remember your positions and cues. Ask Mr. Prompter if you don't. Very well, the orchestra has stopped, the front scene opens, and Act I begins … in the drawing room of Trenchard Manor.

(The lights change for the performance, coming up on the furniture and setting that has just been assembled. BUDDI-COMBE sits reading a newspaper, SKILLET dusts as MR. BINNY arranges chairs.)

SKILLET. What a strange house this is.

BUDDICOMBE. Very uncomfortable; I have no curtain to my bed.

SKILLET. And no wine at the second table.

BUDDICOMBE. I'm afraid Sir Edward is in dire straits.

MR. BINNY *(making BUDDICOMBE get up)*. Mind your h'own business instead h'of your betters'. I'm disgusted with you lower servants.

SKILLET. Last year's milliner's bills have not been paid.

BUDDICOMBE. Miss Florence has had no new dresses from London all winter.

MR. BINNY. That'll do; that'll do! Remember, to check h'idle curiosity is the first duty of men in livery. Ha, here h'are the letters.

(Enter JOHN WICKENS, the gardener, with green bag. MR. BINNY takes the bag, removes letters and reads addresses.)

MR. BINNY. Miss Augusta, Mrs. Mountchessington, Lord Dundreary. Miss Georgina Mountchessington, Lieut. Vernon. Ah! that's from the admiralty. What's this? Miss Florence Trenchard via Brattleboro, Vermont.

BUDDICOMBE. Where's that, Mr. Binny?

JOHN. Why, that be h'in the United States of North H'america, and a good place for poor folks.

MR. BINNY. John Wickens, you forget yourself.

JOHN. Beg pardon, Mr. Binny.

MR. BINNY. John Wickens, leave the room!

JOHN. But I know where Vermont be, though. *(Making a face, he goes out.)*

BUDDICOMBE *(looking at letter in MR. BINNY's hand).* Why, that is Master Ned's hand, Mr. Binny. He must have been sporting in Vermont.

MR. BINNY. Yes, no doubt shooting the wild h'elephants and buffaloes what abound there.

BUDDICOMBE. The nasty beasts! *(Looking off.)* Hello, here comes Miss Florence tearing across the lane like a three-year-old colt.

(FLORENCE [LAURA KEENE] enters running.)

FLORENCE. Oh! I'm fairly out of breath! Good morning, Binny. I saw Wickens coming with the letter bag. I thought I could catch him before I reached the house. So off I started, but I forgot the pond, and it was in or over. I got over; but my hat got in. I wish you'd fish it out for me. You won't find the pond very deep.

MR. BINNY. Me fish for an 'at? Does she take me for an h'angler?

FLORENCE. Give me the letters. *(Looks through them.)* Bills! Blessed budget that descends upon Trenchard Manor like rain on a duck pond. *(To MR. BINNY.)* Tell Papa and all, that the letters have come. You will find them on the terrace.

MR. BINNY. Yes, miss.

FLORENCE. And then go fish my hat out of the pond. It's not very deep.

MR. BINNY. Me fish for 'ats? She does take me for an h'angler. *(Exits, disgusted.)*

FLORENCE *(looking at letters again).* "Lieut. Vernon. In Her Majesty's service. Admiralty, R.N." Ah, that's an answer to Harry's application for a ship. Papa promised to use his influence for him. I hope he has succeeded. But then he will have to leave us, and who knows if he ever comes back. What a foolish girl I am, when I know that his rise in the service will depend upon it. I do hope he'll get it, and if he must leave us, I'll bid him goodbye as a lass who loves a sailor should.

(SIR EDWARD, MRS. MOUNTCHESSINGTON, AUGUS-TA, and VERNON enter, in conversation.)

FLORENCE. Papa, dear, here are letters for you. One for you, Mrs. Mountchessington. And for you, Harry. *(Hides the letter behind her.)*

VERNON. Ah, one for me, Florence?

FLORENCE. Now what will you give me for one?

VERNON *(kissing her)*. Ah, then you have one?

FLORENCE. Yes, here, Harry.

VERNON. Ah, for a ship. *(Opens and reads the letter.)*

FLORENCE. Ah! *Mon ami*, you are to leave us? Good news, or bad?

VERNON. No ship yet. This promises another year of land-lubbery.

FLORENCE. I'm so sorry. *(To herself.)* I'm so glad he's not going away. But where's Dundreary? Has anybody seen Dundreary?

(LORD DUNDREARY [MR. EMERSON] enters, walks about the room, employing his hop.)

DUNDREARY. Good morning, Miss Florence.

FLORENCE. Good morning, my Lord Dundreary. Who do you think has been here? What does the postman bring?

DUNDREARY. Well, sometimes he brings a bag with a lock on it, sometimes newspapers, and sometimes letters, I suppothe.

FLORENCE. There. *(Gives DUNDREARY a letter, which he has difficulty in opening. FLORENCE helps him.)*

DUNDREARY. That's the idea! Thank you!

AUGUSTA. Florence, dear, here's a letter of yours got among mine. *(Gives it to her.)*

FLORENCE. Why, Papa, it's from dear brother Ned.

SIR EDWARD. From my boy! Where is he? How is he? Read it!

FLORENCE. He writes from Brattleboro, Vermont. *(Reads.)* "Quite well, just come in from a shooting excursion. With a party of Crows, splendid fellows. Six feet high."

DUNDREARY. Birds six feet high—what tremendous animals they must be!

FLORENCE. Oh, I see what my brother means; a tribe of Indians called Crows. Not birds. *(Reads from letter.)* "By the bye, I have lately come quite haphazard upon the other branch of our family, which emigrated to America at the Restoration. They are now thriving in this state and, discovering our relationship, they received me most hospitably. I have cleared up the mysterious death of old Mark Trenchard."

SIR EDWARD. Of my uncle!

FLORENCE. "It appears that when he quarreled with his daughter on her marriage with poor Meredith, he came here in search of this stray shoot of the family tree, found them and died in their house, leaving Asa, one of the sons, heir to his personal property in England, which ought to belong to poor Mary Meredith. Asa is about to sail for the old country, to take possession. I gave him directions to seek you out, and he should arrive almost as soon as this letter. Receive him kindly for the sake of the kindness he has shown to me, and let him see some of our shooting. Your affectionate brother, Ned."

SIR EDWARD. An American branch of the family?

MRS. MOUNTCHESSINGTON. Oh, how interesting!

AUGUSTA. How delightfully romantic! I can imagine the wild young hunter. An Apollo of the prairie.

FLORENCE. An Apollo of the prairie? Yes, with a strong nasal twang, and a decided taste for tobacco and cobblers.

DUNDREARY. Florence, you forget that he is a Trenchard, and no true Trenchard would have a liking for cobblers or low people of that kind.

FLORENCE. I hate him, whatever he is. Coming here to rob poor cousin Mary of her grandmother's guineas.

SIR EDWARD. Florence, how often must I request you not to speak of Mary Meredith as your cousin?

FLORENCE. Why, she is my cousin, is she not? Besides, she presides over her milk pail like a duchess playing dairymaid. And I am so fond of my cousin's sillabubs. Dundreary, do you know what sillabubs are?

DUNDREARY. Oh, yeth, I know what a sillabub is. Yeth! Yeth!

FLORENCE. Why, I don't believe you do know what it is.

DUNDREARY. Not know what sillabubs are? That's a good idea. Why, they are—sillabubs are—they are silly babies, idiotic children. That's a good idea, that's good. *(Bumps his head against FLORENCE.)*

FLORENCE. No, it's not a bit like the idea. What you mean are called cherubims.

DUNDREARY. What, those things that look like oranges, with wings on them?

FLORENCE. Not a bit like it. Well, after luncheon you must go with me and I'll introduce you to my cousin Mary and sillabubs.

DUNDREARY. I never saw Mr. Sillabubs, I am sure.

FLORENCE. Sillabubs, dear sir, a dish made of wine and cream! You shall see. Well, now, don't forget.

DUNDREARY. I never forget—when I can recollect.

FLORENCE. Then recollect that you have an appointment with me after luncheon.

DUNDREARY. Yeth, yeth.

FLORENCE. Well, what have you after luncheon?

DUNDREARY. Well, sometimes I have a glass of brandy with an egg in it, sometimes a run around the duck pond, sometimes a game of checkers—that's for exercise, and sometimes a game of billiards.

FLORENCE. No, no! You have with me after luncheon, an ap—an ap—

DUNDREARY. An ap—an ap—

FLORENCE. An ap—an appoint—appointment.

DUNDREARY. An ointment, that's the idea!

MRS. MOUNTCHESSINGTON *(whispering to AUGUSTA)*. That artful girl has designs upon Lord Dundreary. Augusta, dear, go and see how your poor, dear sister, Georgina, is this morning.

AUGUSTA. Yes, Mamma. *(Goes out.)*

MRS. MOUNTCHESSINGTON. Georgina is a great sufferer, my dear.

DUNDREARY. Yeth, but a lonely one.

FLORENCE. What sort of night had she?

MRS. MOUNTCHESSINGTON. Oh, a very refreshing one, thanks to the draught you were kind enough to prescribe for her, Lord Dundreary.

FLORENCE. What! Has Lord Dundreary been prescribing for Georgina?

DUNDREARY. Yeth, you see I gave her a draught that cured the effect of the draught, and that draught was a draught that didn't pay the doctor's bill. Didn't that draught—

FLORENCE. Good gracious! What a number of draughts. You have almost a game of draughts.

DUNDREARY. Ha! Ha! Ha! *(Doubles over in laughter.)*

FLORENCE. What's the matter?

DUNDREARY. That wath a joke, that wath!

FLORENCE. Where's the joke?

DUNDREARY. She don't see it. Don't you see—a game of draughts—pieces of wound wood on square pieces of leather. That's the idea! Now, I want to ask you a *whime*!

FLORENCE. A *whime*, what's that?

DUNDREARY. A *whime* is a *widdle*, you know.

FLORENCE. A *widdle*!

DUNDREARY. Yeth, one of those things, like—why is so and so on somebody like somebody else?

FLORENCE. Oh, I see, you mean a conundrum.

DUNDREARY. Yeth, a drum, that's the idea! What is it gives a cold in the head, cures a cold, pays a doctor's bill and makes the home guard look for substitutes? *(FLORENCE repeats the riddle.)* Yeth, do you give up?

FLORENCE. Yes.

DUNDREARY. Well, I'll tell you—a draught. *(FLORENCE alone politely laughs.)* Now, I've got a better one than that. When is a dog's tail not a dog's tail? *(FLORENCE repeats it.)* Yeth, that's a stunner. You've got to give that up.

FLORENCE. Yes, and willingly.

DUNDREARY. When it's a cart. *(Everyone looks at him with puzzled expressions.)*

FLORENCE. Why, what on earth has a dog's tail to do with a cart?

DUNDREARY. When it moves about, you know. A horse makes a cart move; so does a dog make his tail move.

FLORENCE. I see what you mean—when it's a wagon. *(Wags the letter in her hand in front of DUNDREARY. Everyone laughs.)*

DUNDREARY. Well, a wagon and a cart are the same thing, ain't they? That's the idea—it's the same thing.

FLORENCE. They are not the same. In the case of your conundrum, there's a very great difference.

DUNDREARY. Now I've got another. Why does a dog waggle his tail?

FLORENCE. Upon my word, I never inquired.

DUNDREARY. Because the tail can't waggle the dog. Ha! Ha!

FLORENCE *(forcing a laugh)*. Ha! Ha! Is that your own, Dundreary?

DUNDREARY. Now I've got one, and this one is original.

FLORENCE. No, no, don't spoil the last one.

DUNDREARY. Yeth, but this is extremely interesting.

MRS. MOUNTCHESSINGTON. Do you think so, Lord Dundreary?

DUNDREARY. Yeth. Miss Georgina likes me to tell her my jokes. By the bye, talking of the lonely sufferer, isn't she an interesting invalid? They do say that's what's the matter with me. I'm an interesting invalid.

FLORENCE. Oh, that accounts for what I have heard so many young ladies say—"Florence, dear, don't you think Lord Dundreary's extremely interesting?" I never knew what they meant before.

DUNDREARY. Yeth, the doctor recommends me to drink donkey's milk.

FLORENCE *(hiding her laughter)*. Oh, what a clever man he must be. He knows we generally thrive best on our native food.

DUNDREARY. I'm so weak, and that's so strong. Yes, I'm naturally very weak, and I want strengthening. Yes, I guess I'll try it. *(Looks off.)* Look at this lovely sufferer.

(DUNDREARY welcomes GEORGINA, an uncommonly large girl, who is followed by her sister, AUGUSTA.)

DUNDREARY *(seating GEORGINA)*. There, repothe yourself.

GEORGINA *(fanning herself)*. Thank you, my lord. Everybody is kind to me, and I am so delicate.

SIR EDWARD *(looking up from his letters)*. Florence, dear, I must leave you to represent me to my guests. These letters will give me a great deal of business today.

FLORENCE. Well, Papa, remember I am your little clerk and person of all work.

SIR EDWARD. No, no, this is private business—money matters, my love, which women know nothing about. Luckily for them. I expect Mr. Coyle today.

FLORENCE. Dear Papa, how I wish you would get another agent.

SIR EDWARD. Nonsense, Florence, impossible. He knows my affairs; his father was for the late Baronet. He's one of the family, almost.

FLORENCE. Papa, I have implicit faith in my own judgment of faces. Depend upon it, that man is not to be trusted.

SIR EDWARD. Florence, you are ridiculous. I could not get on a week without him. Curse him, I wish I could! Coyle is a most intelligent man, and a most faithful servant of the family.

(MR. BINNY enters.)

MR. BINNY. Mr. Coyle and h'agent with papers.

SIR EDWARD. Show him into the library. I will be with him presently. *(MR. BINNY goes out.)*

FLORENCE. Remember the archery meeting, Papa. It's at three.

SIR EDWARD. Yes, yes, I'll remember. *(To himself.)* Pretty time for such levity when ruin stares me in the face. Florence, I leave you as my representative. *(To himself.)* Now to prepare myself to meet my Shylock. *(Goes out.)*

FLORENCE. Why will Papa not trust me? Oh, Harry! I wish he would find out what a lot of pluck and common sense there is in this feather head of mine.

DUNDREARY. Miss Florence, will you be kind enough to tell Miss Georgina all about that American relative of yours?

FLORENCE. Oh, about my American cousin, certainly. *(Whispers to VERNON.)* Let's have some fun. *(Then aloud.)* Well, he's about seventeen feet high.

DUNDREARY. Good gracious! Seventeen feet high!

FLORENCE. They all are seventeen feet high in America, aren't they, Mr. Vernon?

VERNON. Yes, that's about the average height.

FLORENCE. And they have long black hair that reaches down to their heels, they have dark copper-colored skin, and they fight with—what do they fight with, Mr. Vernon?

VERNON. Tomahawks and scalping knives.

FLORENCE. Yes, and you'd better take care, Miss Georgina, or he'll take his tomahawk and scalping knife and scalp you immediately. *(GEORGINA screams and faints.)*

DUNDREARY. Here, somebody get something and throw over her. A pail of water! No, not that, she's pale enough already. *(Fans her with handkerchief.)* Georgina, don't be afraid. Dundreary's by your side; he will protect you. *(GEORGINA revives.)*

FLORENCE. Don't be frightened, Georgina. Our American cousin will never harm you while Dundreary is about. Why, he could get three scalps here. *(Pulls DUNDREARY's whiskers. GEORGINA screams.)*

DUNDREARY. Don't scream. I won't lose my whiskers. I know what I'll do for my own safety. I will take this handkerchief and tie the roof of my head on. *(Puts handkerchief on his head and ties it under his chin.)*

FLORENCE *(pretending to cry)*. Goodbye, Dundreary. I'll never see you again in all your glory.

DUNDREARY. Don't cry, Miss Florence, I'm ready for Mr. Tommy Hawk.

(Enter MR. BINNY.)

MR. BINNY. If you please, miss. 'Ere's a gent what says he's h'expected.

FLORENCE. What's his name? Where's his card?

MR. BINNY. He didn't tell me his name, miss, and when I h'axed him for his card had a whole pack in his valise, and he asked me if I had in mind to play a game of seven h'up. He says he has come to stay, and he certainly looks as if he didn't mean to go.

FLORENCE. That's him. Show him in, Mr. Binny. That's our American cousin, I know. *(MR. BINNY goes out.)*

AUGUSTA *(romantically)*. Our American cousin! Oh, how delightfully romantic, isn't it? I can imagine the wild young hunter, with the free step and majestic mien of the hunter of the forest.

ASA *(offstage)*. Didn't I tell you I was expected?

(ASA TRENCHARD, "our American cousin," enters, carrying his valise. He is followed by an exasperated BINNY.)

ASA. Where's the squire?

FLORENCE. Do you mean Sir Edward Trenchard, sir?

ASA. Yes.

FLORENCE. He is not present, but I am his daughter.

ASA. Well, I guess that'll fit about as well if you tell the darned old shoat to take me to my room.

FLORENCE. What does he mean by shoat?

MR. BINNY *(taking valise)*. He means me, mum; but what he wants—

ASA. Hurry up, old hoss!

MR. BINNY. He calls me a 'oss, miss; I suppose I shall be a h'ox next, or perhaps an 'og.

ASA. Wal, darn me, if you ain't the consarnedest old shoat I ever did see since I was baptized Asa Trenchard.

FLORENCE. Ah! Then it is our American cousin! Glad to see you. My brother told us to expect you.

ASA. Wal, yes, I guess you do belong to my family. I'm Asa Trenchard, born in Vermont, suckled on the banks of Muddy Creek, about the tallest gunner, the slickest dancer and generally the loudest critter in the state. You're my cousin, be you? Wal, I ain' t got no objections to kiss you, as one cousin ought to kiss another. *(Approaches her.)*

VERNON. Sir, how dare you?

ASA. Are you one of the family? 'Cause if you ain't, you've got no right to interfere, and if you be, you needn't be alarmed, I ain't going to kiss you. Here's your young man's letter. *(Gives FLORENCE letter and attempts to kiss her.)*

FLORENCE. In the old country, Mr. Trenchard, cousins content themselves with hands, but our hearts are with them. You are welcome, there is mine. *(Gives her hand, which he shakes heartily.)*

ASA. That'll do about as well. I won't kiss you if you don't want me to; but if you did, I wouldn't stop on account of that sailor man. *(To VERNON.)* Oh! Now you needn't get your back up. What an all-fired chap you are. Now if you'll have me shown to my room, I should like to fix up a bit and put on a clean buzzom. *(All start.)* Why, what on earth is the matter with you all? I only spoke because you're so all-fired go-to-meeting like.

FLORENCE. Show Mr. Trenchard to the red room, Mr. Binny. That is, if you are done with it, Dundreary.

DUNDREARY. Yeth, Miss Florence. The room and I have got through with each other, yeth. *(ASA and DUNDREARY see each other for the first time.)*

ASA *(pointing at DUNDREARY)*. Concentrated essence of baboons, what on earth is that?

DUNDREARY. He's mad. Yeth, Miss Florence, I've done with that room. The birds crowed so that they racked my brain.

ASA. You don't mean to say that you've got any brains.

DUNDREARY. No, sir, such a thing never entered my head.

FLORENCE. The red room, then, Mr. Binny.

ASA *(to MR. BINNY)*. Hold on! *(Examining him.)* Wal, darn me, but you keep your help in all-fired good order here. This old shoat is fat enough to kill. *(Hits MR. BINNY in stomach. MR. BINNY runs off.)* Mind how you go up stairs, old hoss, or you'll bust your biler. *(Follows MR. BINNY out.)*

DUNDREARY. Now he thinks Binny's an engine, and has got a boiler.

FLORENCE. Oh, what fun!

MRS. MOUNTCHESSINGTON. Old Mark Trenchard died very rich, did he not, Florence?

FLORENCE. Very rich, I believe.

AUGUSTA. Asa's not at all romantic, is he, Mamma?

MRS. MOUNTCHESSINGTON *(whispering to her)*. My dear, I have no doubt he has solid good qualities, and I don't want you to laugh at him like Florence Trenchard.

AUGUSTA. No, Mamma, I won't.

FLORENCE. But what are we to do with him?

DUNDREARY. Ha! Ha! Ha!

ALL. What is the matter?

DUNDREARY. I've got an idea.

FLORENCE. Oh? Let's hear Dundreary's idea.

DUNDREARY. It's so seldom I get an idea that when I do get one it startles me. Let us get a pickle bottle.

FLORENCE. Pickle bottle?

DUNDREARY. Yeth, one of those things with glass sides.

(ASA enters but is not seen by DUNDREARY.)

FLORENCE. You mean a glass case?

DUNDREARY. Yeth, a glass case, that's the idea, and let us put this Mr. Thomas Hawk in it, and have him on exhibition. That's the idea!

ASA *(overhearing)*. Oh! That's your idea, is it? Wal, stranger, I don't know what they're going to do with me, but wherever they do put me, I hope it will be out of the reach of a jackass. I'm a real hoss, I am, and I get kinder riley with those critters.

DUNDREARY. Now he thinks he's a horse. I've heard of a great jackass, and I dreamt of a jackass, but I don't believe there is any such insect.

FLORENCE. Well, cousin, I hope you made yourself comfortable.

ASA. Wal, no, I can't say as I did. You see, there were so many all-fired fixin's in my room I couldn't find anything I wanted.

FLORENCE. What was it you couldn't find in your room?

ASA. There was no soft soap.

AUGUSTA. Soft soap!

VERNON. Soft soap?

MRS. MOUNTCHESSINGTON. Soft soap!

FLORENCE. Soft soap?

GEORGINA. Soft soap!

DUNDREARY. Thoft thoap?

ASA. Yes, soft soap. I reckon you know what that is. However, I struck a pump in the kitchen, slicked my hair down a little, gave my boots a lick of grease, and now I feel quite handsome. But I'm everlastingly dry.

FLORENCE. You'll find ale, wine, and luncheon on the side table.

ASA. Wal, I don't know as I've got any appetite. You see, comin' along on the cars I worried down half a dozen ham sandwiches, eight or ten boiled eggs, two or three pumpkin pies, and a string of cold sausages. Wal, I guess I can hold on till dinnertime.

DUNDREARY. Did the illustrious exile eat all that? I wonder where he put it.

(MR. BINNY rolls in luncheon table.)

ASA. I'm as dry as a sap-tree in August.

MR. BINNY. Luncheon!

ASA *(looking over luncheon)*. Wal, I don't want to speak out too plain, but this is an awful mean set-out for a big house like this.

FLORENCE. Why, what's wrong, sir?

ASA. Why, there's no mush!

DUNDREARY. No mush?

ASA. Nor any slapjack.

DUNDREARY. Why, does he want to slap Jack?

ASA. No pork and beans!

DUNDREARY. Pork's been here, but he's left.

ASA. And where on airth's the clam chowder?

DUNDREARY. Where is clam chowder? He's never here when he's wanted.

ASA *(taking a drink and spitting)*. Here's your health, old hoss. Do you call that a drink? See here, cousin, you seem to be the liveliest critter here, so just hurry up the fixin's, and I'll show this benighted aristocratic society what real liquor is. So hurry up the fixin's.

ALL. Fixin's?

FLORENCE. What do you mean by fixin's?

ASA. Why, brandy, gin and whiskey. We'll make them all useful.

FLORENCE. Oh, I'll hurry up the fixin's! What fun! *(Goes out.)*

DUNDREARY. Oh! I thought he meant the gas fixin's.

ASA. Say, you, you Mr. Puffy, you run out and get me a bunch of mint and a bundle of straws. Hurry up, old hoss! *(MR. BINNY hurries out.)* Say, Mr. Sailor man, just help me down this table. Oh! Don't you get riley; you and I ran against each other when I came in, but we'll be friends yet. *(VERNON helps him with table.)*

(FLORENCE enters, followed by servants who carry a case of decanters, on which are seven or eight glasses, two or three tin mixers and a bowl of sugar. MR. BINNY enters with a bunch of mint and a few straws.)

FLORENCE. Here, cousin, are the fixin's.

ASA. That's yer sort. Now then, I'll give you all a drink that'll make you squeal. *(To MR. BINNY.)* Here, Puffy, just shake that up faster. I'll give that sick gal a drink that'll make her squirm like an eel on a mudbank.

DUNDREARY *(screaming)*. What a horrible idea! *(Hops about stage.)*

FLORENCE. Oh, don't mind him! That's only an American joke, Lord Dundreary.

DUNDREARY. A joke! Do you call that a joke? To make a sick girl squirm like a mudbank on an eel?

ASA. Yes, I'll give you a drink that'll make your whiskers

return under your chin, which is their natural location. Now, ladies and gentlemen, what'll you have: Whiskey Skin, Brandy Smash, Sherry Cobbler, Mint Julep or Jersey Lightning?

AUGUSTA. Oh. I want a Mint Julep.

FLORENCE. I'll take a Sherry Cobbler.

VERNON. Brandy Smash for me.

MRS. MOUNTCHESSINGTON. Give me a Whiskey Skin.

GEORGINA. I'll take a lemonade.

DUNDREARY. Give me a Jersey Lightning.

ASA. Give him a Jersey Lightning. *(Mixes a special drink which fizzes and foams.)* Warranted to kill at forty rods.

(As everyone watches, DUNDREARY takes the drink from ASA, holds it high, and drinks it down. Promptly he falls over full length at the feet of MRS. MOUNTCHESSING-TON and GEORGINA. Everyone reacts to DUNDREARY, and holds his position. The lights fade on the scene, and remain dim for the interlude. When LAURA KEENE speaks, the actors break their positions. The stagehands come in and change the furniture arrangement for the next scene.)

LAURA KEENE. That played quite freshly, I think. We won't need to repeat any part of it, I am happy to say. You may proceed with the second scene, Mr. Prompter.

PROMPTER. Mr. Binny and Mr. Coyle, please. The scene, the Library in the Trenchard Manor, is open. You enter, please.

(They do so.)

MR. BINNY. Sir H'edward will see you directly, Mr. Coyle.

MR. COYLE. Very well. House full of company, I see, Mr. Binny.

MR. BINNY. Cram full, Mr. Coyle. As one of the first families in the country, we must keep up our position.

MR. COYLE *(rubbing his hands).* Certainly, certainly! That is, as long as we can, Mr. Binny. Tell Murcott, my clerk, to bring my papers in here. You'll find him in the servants' hall. And see that you keep your strong ale out of his way. People who serve me must have their senses about them.

MR. BINNY *(to himself).* I should say so, or 'e'd 'ave every tooth h'out in their 'eads, the wiper. *(Goes out.)*

MR. COYLE. And now to show this pompous baronet the precipice on which he stands.

(MR. MURCOTT enters, carrying bag and papers.)

MR. COYLE. Are you sober, sirrah?

MR. MURCOTT. Yes, Mr. Coyle.

MR. COYLE. Then see you keep so.

MR. MURCOTT. I'll do my best, sir. But, oh, do tell them to keep liquor out of my way. I can't keep from it now, try as I will, and I try hard enough, God help me!

MR. COYLE. Pshaw! Get out those mortgages and the letters from my London agent. *(MURCOTT takes papers from bag and places them on table. COYLE looks off.)* So. Here comes Sir Edward. Go, but be within call. I may want you to witness a signature.

MR. MURCOTT. I will, sir. I must have brandy, or my hand will not be steady enough to write. *(Goes out.)*

(SIR EDWARD enters; MR. COYLE bows.)

SIR EDWARD. Good morning, Coyle, good morning. *(With affected ease.)* There is a chair, Coyle. *(They sit.)* So, you see, these infernal tradespeople are pretty troublesome.

MR. COYLE. My agent's letter this morning announces that Walters and Brass have got judgment and execution on their amount for repairing your town house last season.

(Refers to papers.) Boquet and Barker announce their intention of taking this same course with the wine account. Hardmarth is preparing …

SIR EDWARD. Confound it, why harass me with details, these infernal particulars! Have you made out the total?

MR. COYLE. Four thousand, eight hundred and sixty pounds, nine shillings and sixpence.

SIR EDWARD. Well, of course, we must find means of settling this extortion.

MR. COYLE. Yes, Sir Edward, if possible.

SIR EDWARD. If possible? Why, you don't say there will be any difficulty in raising the money?

MR. COYLE. What means would you suggest, Sir Edward?

SIR EDWARD. That, sir, is your business.

MR. COYLE. How, Sir Edward?

SIR EDWARD. Confound it, sir, which of us is the agent? Am I to find you brains for your own business?

MR. COYLE. No, Sir Edward, I can furnish the brains, but what I ask of you is to furnish the money.

SIR EDWARD. There must be money somewhere. I came into possession of one of the finest properties in Hampshire only twenty-six years ago, and now you mean to tell me I cannot raise four thousand pounds?

MR. COYLE. The fact is distressing, Sir Edward, but it is so.

SIR EDWARD. There's the Ravensdale property unencumbered.

MR. COYLE. There, Sir Edward, you are under a mistake. The Ravensdale property is deeply encumbered, to nearly its full value.

SIR EDWARD *(springing up)*. Good heavens!

MR. COYLE. I have found among my father's papers a mortgage of that very property to him.

SIR EDWARD. To your father? My father's agent? A mortgage on the Ravensdale estate? But it must have been paid off, Mr. Coyle. *(Anxiously.)* Have you looked for the release or the receipt?

MR. COYLE. Neither exists. My father's sudden death explains sufficiently. I was left in ignorance of the transaction; but the seals on the deed and the stamps are intact. Here it is, sir. *(Shows it.)*

SIR EDWARD *(sinking down into chair)*. Sir, do you know that if this be true I am something like a beggar, and your father something like a thief?

MR. COYLE. I see the first plainly, Sir Edward, but not the second.

SIR EDWARD. Do you forget, sir, that your father was a charity boy, fed, clothed, by my father?

MR. COYLE. Pardon me, sir. You have only to repay the money and the estate is yours.

SIR EDWARD. How dare you, sir, when you have just shown me that I cannot raise five hundred pounds in the world! Oh! Florence, why did I not listen to you when you warned me against this man?

MR. COYLE *(to himself)*. Oh? She warned you, did she? *(To SIR EDWARD.)* I see one means, at least, of keeping the Ravensdale estate in the family.

SIR EDWARD. What is it?

MR. COYLE. By marrying your daughter to the mortgagee.

SIR EDWARD. To you?

MR. COYLE. I am prepared to settle the estate on Miss Trenchard the day she becomes Mrs. Richard Coyle.

SIR EDWARD *(springing up)*. You insolent scoundrel, how dare you insult me in my own house, sir! Leave it, sir, or I will have you removed by my servants.

MR. COYLE. I never take an angry man at his word, Sir Edward. Give a few moments' reflection to my offer, and you can have me kicked out afterwards. *(Turns away.)*

SIR EDWARD *(to himself)*. To see my children reduced to labor for their bread, to misery perhaps. But the alternative: Florence detests him. Still, the match would save her, at least, from ruin.

MR. COYLE. Now, Sir Edward, shall I ring for the servants to kick me out?

SIR EDWARD. Nay, Mr. Coyle, you must pardon my outburst, you know I am hasty, and—

FLORENCE *(calling from offstage)*. Papa, dear.

(FLORENCE enters gaily, and starts on seeing COYLE.)

FLORENCE. Papa, pardon my breaking in on business, but our American cousin has come—such an original—and we are only waiting for you to escort us to the field.

SIR EDWARD. I will come directly, my love. Mr. Coyle, my dear, you did not see him.

FLORENCE. Oh! Yes, I saw him, Papa. *(Turns away.)*

SIR EDWARD. Florence, your hand to Mr. Coyle. I insist.

FLORENCE. Papa! *(Frightened by his look, she gives her hand. COYLE attempts to kiss it; she snatches it away.)*

SIR EDWARD. Come, Florence. Mr. Coyle, we will join you in the park. Come, my love, take my arm. *(Hurries her off.)*

MR. COYLE. Shallow, selfish fool! She warned you of me, did she? And you did not heed her; you shall both pay dearly. She, for her suspicions, and you that you did not heed them. *(Walks up and down.)* How lucky the seals were not cut from that mortgage when the release was given. This mortgage makes Ravensdale mine, while the release that restores it to its owner lies in the recess of the bureau, whose secret my father revealed to me on his death bed.

(MR. MURCOTT enters.)

MR. COYLE. Write to the mortgagee of the Fanhill and El-
lenthorpe estates to foreclose before the week is out, and
tell Walters and Brass to put in execution today. Abel, we
both have a bone to pick with him and his daughter. *(MUR-
COTT starts.)* Why, what's the matter?

MR. MURCOTT. Nothing; the dizziness I've had lately.

MR. COYLE. Brandy in the evening, brandy in the morning,
brandy all night. What a fool you are, Murcott!

MR. MURCOTT. Who knows as well as I do?

MR. COYLE. If you would but keep the money out of your
mouth, there's the making of a man in you yet.

MR. MURCOTT. No, no, it's gone too far; it's gone too far,
thanks to the man who owns this house. You know all about
it. How he found me a thriving, sober lad, flogging the vil-
lage children through their spelling book. How he took a
fancy to me, as he called it, and employed me here to teach
his son and Miss Florence. *(Voice falters.)* Then remember
how I forgot who and what I was, and was cuffed out of the
house like a dog. How I lost my school, my good name, but
still hung about the place. They all looked askance at me—
you don't know how that kills the heart of a man. Then I
took to drink and sank down, down, till I came to this.

MR. COYLE. You owe Sir Edward revenge, do you not? You
shall have a rare revenge on him. That mortgage you found
last week puts the rest of the property in my reach, and I
close my hand on it unless he will consent to my terms.

MR. MURCOTT. You can drive a hard bargain. I know.

MR. COYLE. A rare price I ask for his forbearance, Abel—
his daughter's hand.

MR. MURCOTT. Florence?

MR. COYLE. Yes, Florence marries Richard Coyle. Richard
Coyle steps into Sir Edward's estates. Will not that be a rare
revenge? *(Goes out.)*

MR. MURCOTT. He marry Florence? Florence Trenchard? My Florence. Mine! Florence his wife? No, no, better a thousand times she had been mine, low as I am. It shan't be; it shan't be. I can help her, sot though I am. Yes, I can help her, if the shock don't break me down. Oh! My poor muddled brain, surely there was a release with it when I found it. I must see Florence to warn her and expose Coyle's villainy. Oh! how my poor head throbs. I shall die if I don't have a drop of brandy; yes, brandy! *(Holds his head in pain.)*

(The lights change on the scene as LAURA KEENE comes forth.)

LAURA KEENE. Murcott, one point you overlooked. Remember when you say, "It shan't be; it shan't be," you are to put the papers in the bag with great trembling?

MR. MURCOTT. I clean forgot; I'm sorry, Miss Keene. I've been wondering, would it be possible to have real brandy in this scene?

LAURA KEENE. No, no, no! You and Mr. Emerson are convincing enough as it is. *(Hurries off, leaving MURCOTI to gather up his papers and leave the stage.)*

(The stagehands change the setting. The PROMPTER places several props and checks them on a list he carries.)

PROMPTER. Bottle in table drawer. Valise on floor. *(Places these.)*

ASA *(to PROMPTER).* Have you got my cigar handy?

PROMPTER. Get in place and I'll light it for you. *(Takes cigar out of his pocket and lights it.)* Mr. Binny, in your place, please.

ASA. The bottle in the table?

PROMPTER. It's set. We're ready, Miss Keene.

LAURA KEENE *(from offstage)*. Continue, please.

(Lights come up on the scene: ASA's bedroom at Trenchard Manor. A large shower bath has been rolled in. ASA is seated with foot on table, smoking cigar. MR. BINNY is standing by his side.)

ASA. Wal, I guess I begin to feel kinder comfortable here in this place, if it wasn't for this 'tarnal critter. He doesn't seem to have any work to do, but swells out his big bosom like an old turkey cock in laying time. I do wonder what he's here for. Do they think I mean to absquatulate with the spoons? *(MR. BINNY attempts to take valise, ASA puts his foot on it.)*

MR. BINNY. Will you have the kindness to give me your keys, h'if you please, sir?

ASA. What do you want with my keys?

MR. BINNY. To put your things away in the wardrobe, sir.

ASA. Wal, I calculate if my two shirts, three bosoms, four collars, and two pair of socks were to get into that ever lasting big bunk, they'd think themselves so all-fired small I should never be able to crawl into them again.

MR. BINNY. Will you take a baath before you dress?

ASA. Take a baath?

MR. BINNY. A baath.

ASA. I suppose you mean a bath. Wal, man, I calculate I ain't going to expose myself to the shakes by getting into cold water in this cruel cold climate of yours, so make tracks.

MR. BINNY. Make what?

ASA. Vamose?

MR. BINNY. Make vamose?

ASA. Absquatulate.

MR. BINNY. Ab—what, sir?

ASA. Skedaddle.

MR. BINNY. Skedaddle?

ASA. Oh! Get out.

MR. BINNY. Oh! *(Going.)* If you are going to dress, you'll want some assistance.

ASA. Assistance? What, to get out of my unmentionables and into them again? Wal, s'pose I do, what then?

MR. BINNY. Just ring the Bell; I'll attend you.

ASA. All right, come along. *(MR. BINNY is leaving.)* Hold on, I may yawn presently and I shall want someone to shut my mouth. *(MR. BINNY hurries off.)* Wal, now I am alone, I can look about me and indulge the inquiring spirit of a American citizen. What an everlasting lot of things and fixin's there is, to be sure. *(Opens table drawer.)* Hallo, what's this? Something good to drink. *(Smells bottle.)* It seems awful bad. *(Reads label.)* "Golden Fluid, one application turns hair a beautiful brown, several applications will turn the hair a lustrous black." Well, if they keep it on, it may turn a pea green. I reckon this has been left here by some fellow who is ashamed of the natural color of his top knot. *(Knock. ASA replaces bottle in drawer.)* Come in.

(Enter MR. BINNY.)

MR. BINNY. Mr. Buddicombe, sir, my lord's own man.

ASA. Roll him in.

(MR. BINNY beckons, and BUDDICO MBE enters.)

ASA. Turkey cock number two, what is it?

BUDDICOMBE. My Lord Dundreary's compliments—and have you seen a small bottle in the toilet table drawer?

ASA. Suppose I had, what then?

BUDDICOMBE. My lord wants it partic'ly.

ASA. Was it a small bottle?

BUDDICOMBE. A small bottle.

ASA. Blue label?

BUDDICOMBE. Label blue.

ASA. Red sealing wax on the top?

BUDDICOMBE. Red sealing wax.

MR. BINNY. Red wax.

ASA. Nice little bottle?

MR. BINNY. Little bottle nice.

ASA. Wal, I ain't seen it. If my lord sets a value on it, guess it must be worth something.

BUDDICOMBE. Sorry to trouble you, sir.

MR. BINNY. What h'is h'it?

BUDDICOMBE. My lord's hair dye, the last bottle, and he turns red tomorrow. *(Exits in haste.)*

MR. BINNY. 'Orrible? What an h'awful situation, to be sure.

ASA. So I've got my ring on that lord's nose, and if I don't make him dance to my tune, it's a pity.

MR. BINNY. Miss Florence begged me to say she had borrowed a costume for you, for the h'archery meeting, sir.

ASA. H'ain't you dropped something?

MR. BINNY. Where?

ASA. What do you mean by the h'archery meeting?

MR. BINNY. Where they shoot with bows and h'arrows.

ASA. There goes another of them. Oh, you needn't look for them; you can't find 'em when you want 'em. Now you just take my compliments to Miss Trenchard, but when I goes out shooting with injurious weapons I always wears my own genuine shooting costume. That's the natural buff tipped off with a little red paint.

MR. BINNY. Good gracious, he'd look like H'adam and H'eve, in the garden of H'eden. *(Exits.)*

ASA. Wal, there's a queer lot of fixin's. *(Seeing shower bath.)* What on airth is that? Looks like a skeeter net, only it ain't long enough for a feller to lie down in unless he was to coil himself up like a woodchuck in a knothole. I'd just like to know what the all-fired thing is meant for. *(Calls.)* Say, Pufly-Puffy. Oh, he told me if I wanted him to ring the bell. *(Looks around room.)* Where on airth is the bell? Here it is. *(Slips partly inside shower bath, pulls rope; water comes down.)* Murder! Help! Fire! Water! I'm drowned.

(Enter SKILLET, MR. BINNY, and BUDDICOMBE. Seeing ASA, al1 laugh, and keep it up until the scene fades. LAURA KEENE quickly moves onto the stage, giving instructions as she does.)

LAURA KEENE. Skillet, Binny, Buddicombe, one moment, please. You must make certain you keep laughing in this fashion until the Scene is closed. It takes longer here in Washington to close the scene than it did in Baltimore. *(Turning to the PROMPTER.)* Very well, Mr. Prompter, proceed. *(The stagehands change the scenery.)* Bring in the properties in one, please. Mr. Emerson, will you remember your hop? Just as before, please. *(EMERSON does the Dundreary hop for her.)* Splendid! I'm quite certain you'll master it yet.

AUGUSTA. Your bow. *(Hands a bow to MRS. MOUNTCHESSINGTON.)*

MRS. MOUNTCHESSINGTON. Thank you, dear. *(To the PROMPTER.)* We're ready for you.

PROMPTER. Mary, the dairy is over here. Use this chair for the stool, please. Begin.

(The lights come up on MRS. MOUNTCHESSINGTON and AUGUSTA, dressed for Archery Meeting.)

MRS. MOUNTCHESSINGTON. No, my dear Augusta, you must be very careful. I don't by any means want you to give up de Boots. His expectations are excellent. But, pray, be attentive to this American savage, as I rather think he will prove the better match of the two, if what I hear of Mark Trenchard's property be correct.

AUGUSTA *(disinterested)*. Yes, Ma.

MRS. MOUNTCHESSINGTON. And look more cheerful, my love.

AUGUSTA. I am so, so tired, Ma, of admiring things I hate: Captain de Boots and his horses!

MRS. MOUNTCHESSINGTON. Yes, my love, but we are all compelled to make some sacrifices to society. Look at your poor sister, with the appetite.

AUGUSTA. Well, Ma, what must I do about this Yankee?

MRS. MOUNTCHESSINGTON. Well, I think you better read up Dickens' "American Notes." You should know something about George Washington, I suppose.

AUGUSTA *(bored)*. The one with the cherry tree, Ma?

MRS. MOUNTCHESSINGTON. Yes, dear, the Americans are terribly proud of him.

AUGUSTA. Here he comes, Ma. He's such a fright. What a ridiculous figure he looks in that dress. *(Laughs.)*

MRS. MOUNTCHESSINGTON. Hush, my dear.

(ASA enters in archery dress.)

AUGUSTA. Oh, Mr. Trenchard, why did you not bring me one of those lovely Indian's dresses you wear on your boundless prairie?

MRS. MOUNTCHESSINGTON. Yes, one of those dresses in which you hunt the buffalo.

AUGUSTA *(extravagantly)*. Yes, in which you hunt the buffalo.

ASA *(imitating)*. In which I hunt the buffalo. Buffaloes down in Vermont? Wal, you see, them dresses are principally the natural skin, tipped off with paint, and the Indians object to paiting with them.

MRS. MOUNTCHESSINGTON & AUGUSTA. Ahem! Ahem!

ASA. The first buffalo I see about here, I shall hunt up for you.

MRS. MOUNTCHESSINGTON. I suppose we shall see you on the archery ground, Mr. Trenchard?

ASA. Yes. I'll be there like a ton of brick.

AUGUSTA. A ton of brick?

MRS. MOUNTCHESSINGTON. Hush, my dear? That is doubtless some elegant American expression. *(ASA winks at AUGUSTA.)*

AUGUSTA. Ma, he winked at me!

MRS. MOUNTCHESSINGTON. *Au revoir*, Mr. Trenchard!

ASA. Which?

MRS. MOUNTCHESSINGTON. *Au revoir. (Exits with AUGUSTA.)*

ASA *(calling after her)*. No, thank you, don't take any before dinner. *(To himself.)* No use their talking Dutch to me. I feel all tuckered out riding in those cars all night. I'd like to have a snooze if I could find a place to lay down in. *(Sits in the rose bower.)* Hello, somebody coming.

(Enter DUNDREARY, about to sneeze, and BUDDICOMBE.)

BUDDICOMBE. Your lordship!

DUNDREARY. There! No, you've spoiled it.

BUDDICOMBE. Spoiled what, my lord?

DUNDREARY. "Spoiled what, my lord"—why, a most magnificent sneeze!

BUDDICOMBE. I am very sorry, my lord.

DUNDREARY. Now that I can speak alone with you, tell me about that hair dye. Have you found it?

BUDDICOMBE. Not a trace of it, my lord.

DUNDREARY. If you don't find it, I'll discharge you without a character, Buddicombe.

BU DDICOMBE. Very well, my lord. *(Bows and exits.)*

DUNDREARY. He's gone and lost my hair dye. What a dweadful situation to be in. If he don't find it by tomorrow, my whiskers will be bright red. They're a rich brown already. *(Fumbles with his eyeglasses.)* Ah, there's my dear Georgina, that gorgeous creature, that lovely sufferer. I must fly to receive her. *(Goes off.)*

ASA *(looking out)*. He wants a coat of paint awful bad. Here he comes again with the sick girl.

(LORD DUNDR EARY enters with GEORGINA.)

DUNDREARY. Dear lovely sufferer, lean on me.

GEORGINA. Oh, my lord, it is so painful to walk languidly through life, to be unable, at times, to bear the perfumes of one's favorite flowers. Even those violets you sent me yesterday I was compelled to have removed from my room; the perfume was too strong for me. I'm so delicate.

DUNDREARY. Wretched violets!

GEORGINA. I feel I am not long for this world.

DUNDREARY. I like you all the better for that.

GEORGINA. What, my lord?

DUNDREARY. Do you know I'm getting to be very robust?

GEORGINA. Would I could share that fate with you. But I am so delicate.

DUNDREARY. You don't take nourishment enough. You eat like that little bird with the long beak and wings. You know, birds of a feather is worth two in the bush. Let me ask you a widdle: Why does a duck go under water? For di-verse reasons. Now I'll give you another: Why does a duck come out of water? For sundry reasons. You see, you live on suction. You're like that bird with a long bill, they call a doctor. No, that's not it. I thought it was a doctor because it has a long bill. I mean a snipe; yes, you're a lively snipe. Come now, run with me. *(They skip off together.)*

ASA *(looking off)*. There goes a load of wooden nutmegs. Hello, here comes more visitors.

(Enter FLORENCE, with paper.)

FLORENCE *(reading)*. "One who still remembers what he ought long since to have forgotten, wishes to speak with Miss Trenchard"—Florence scratched out—"on matters of life and death, near the dairy." Written upon a dirty sheet of paper, in a hardly legible hand. What does this mean? It opens like one of Mrs. Radcliffe's romances. Well, here I am, now for my correspondent.

(Enter MR. MURCOTT.)

MR. MURCOTT. Oh, for one minute's clear head, Miss Florence.

FLORENCE. I presume you are the writer of this?

MR. MURCOTT. Yes, I am, Miss Florence.

FLORENCE. You address me as an old acquaintance, but I do not recognize you.

MR. MURCOTT. So much the better. So much the better.

FLORENCE. I hate mystery, sir. I must know to whom I am speaking.

MR. MURCOTT. As frank as ever. I am Abel Murcott.

FLORENCE. You?

MR. MURCOTT. Yes, Miss Trenchard. The drunken wretch you see before you once had the audacity to aspire to your hand. Since that fatal day when you rejected me, I have sunk deeper and deeper until I have become what you see me, and now I am indebted for daily bread to your father's agent, Mr. Coyle.

FLORENCE. Mr. Murcott, I am truly sorry to see you thus.

MR. MURCOTT. No, don't pity me. 'Tis not of myself I would speak. I come to tell you of your father's ruin, his utter ruin. His estates are all mortgaged and Mr. Coyle is the principal mortgagee.

FLORENCE. Poor father, what a sad blow for him!

MR. MURCOTT. The worst remains.

FLORENCE. Go on, sir,

MR. MURCOTT. Mr. Coyle promised to release your father from the mortgage of the Ravensdale property, thereby saving him from disgrace—and the price—

FLORENC E. The price, sir?

MR. MU RCOTT. Was your hand in marriage.

FLORENCE. My hand. And my father, how did he listen to such insolence?

MR. MURCOTT. At first, a torrent of rage. Then the ebb of selfishness set in, and he consented to listen to the terms, to view them as something to be considered, to consider them.

FLORENCE. Oh! Where can I look for help? Can you avert this?

ASA (coming out of arbor). Wal, stranger, that's just the question I was going to ask.

FLORE NCE. You here, sir, and listening?

ASA. Wal, it wasn't on purpose. I went in there to take a snooze, I heard you talking, and I thought it wouldn't be polite of me not to listen to what you had to say. I'm a rough sort of customer, and I don't know much about the ways of great folks, but I've a cool head, a stout arm and a willing heart, and I think I can help you, just as one cousin ought to help another.

MR. MURCOTT *(interrupting)*. Shall I go on? I found the Ravensdale mortgage while rummaging in an old deed box of Coyle's father's. There was a folded paper inside the deed. I took both to Coyle unopened, like a besotted fool that I was. My belief is strong that the paper was the release of the mortgage, that the money had been paid off, and the release executed without the seals having been cut from the original mortgage. If you can but find that release, we may unmask this diabolical fiend and save you.

FLORENCE. But, surely, a villain of Coyle's stability would have destroyed the paper, the very keystone of his fraud.

MR. MURCOTT. I fear so.

ASA. Do you, now? Wal, you're wrong, you're both wrong. You ain't either of you done much cyphering human nature. The keystone of their fraud is just the point you mighty cute rascals always leave unsecured. Come along with me, stranger. Two heads are better than one. Yours is a little muddled, but mine's pretty clear, so come along. I mean doing. I do. *(Exits.)*

FLORENCE. Allow me to thank you, Abel, for your warning.

MR. MURCOTT. Don't, oh, don't call me that—for it reminds me of what I was and what I am-and if I reflect on that 'twill drive me mad. Mad! Mad!

(He rushes off, followed by FLORENCE, as JOHN WICK-ENS enters with two milk pails on a yoke. He puts them down and then looks off.)

JOHN. There they go, that's a bull's eye, I warrant. Dang me, though, if I wouldn't rather see Miss Mary than this cock robin sports yonder. Here she comes. Good morning, Miss Mary. *(Enter MARY from dairy cottage.)*

MARY. Oh, Wickens, you are there. How kind of you to help me with the milk pails today, when all the lads and lasses have given themselves a holiday to see the shooting.

JOHN. Ah, Miss Mary, you ought to, be among them, with a green hat and feather, if all had their rights.

MARY *(laughing)*. Nay, ladies without a farthing in the world ought to put aside their ladyships and make themselves; besides, I'm proud of my dairy here. Just help me with this troublesome fellow. Steady, don't shake it, the cream is forming so beautifully. There.

JOHN. Now, Miss Mary, what can I do for you?

MARY. Let me see; well, really, I do believe, Wickens, I've nothing to do but amuse myself.

JOHN. Dang it, miss, that's a pity, because I can't help you at that, you see.

MARY. Oh! Yes, bring me out dear old Welsh nurse's spinning wheel. *(Exit JOHN to cottage.)* By the side of which I have stood so often, a round-eyed baby wondering at its whirring wheel.

(Re-enter JOHN with wheel.)

MARY. There, that will do famously. I can catch the full scent of the jasmines.

JOHN. Anything more, Miss Mary?

MARY. No, thank you, Wickens.

JOHN *(going)*. Good morning, Miss Mary.

MARY. Good morning, Wickens.

JOHN *(returning)*. Is there anything I can get for you, Miss Mary?

MARY *(spinning)*. Nothing, thank you.

JOHN. Dang me if I wouldn't like to stop all day, and watch

her pretty figure and run errands for her. *(After a deep sigh, he exits.)*

MARY. Poor Wickens is not the only one who thinks I am a very ill-used young body. Now I don't think so. Uncle is kind to me in his pompous, patronizing way, and dear Florence loves me like a sister, and so I am happy. I am my own mistress here, and not anybody's humble servant. I sometimes find myself singing as the birds do, because I can't help it. *(Sings.)*

(FLORENCE and ASA enter.)

FLORENCE. Come along, cousin, come along. I want to in troduce you to my little cousin. *(Kisses MARY.)* I've brought you a visitor, Miss Mary Meredith, Mr. Asa Trenchard, our American cousin. *(They shake hands.)* That will do for the present. This young gentleman has carried off the prize by three successive shots in the hull's eye.

MARY. I congratulate you, sir, and am happy to see you.

ASA *(shaking hands again)*. Thank you, miss.

FLORENCE. That will do for a beginning.

ASA. And so this is Mark Trenchard's grandchild.

MARY. Why have you left the archery, Florence?

FLORENCE. Because, after Mr. Asa's display, I felt in no humor for shooting, and I have some very grave business with my cousin here.

MARY. I thought you never had any graver business than being very pretty, very amiable, and very ready to be amused.

ASA. Wal, miss, I guess the first comes natural 'round these diggin's. *(Bows.)*

MARY. You are very polite. This is my domain, sir, and I should be happy to show you; that is, if you understand anything about a dairy.

ASA. Wal, I guess I do know something about cow juice. *(They turn to smother a laugh.)* Why, if it ain't all as bright and clean as a fresh washed shirt just off the clover, and is this all your do in's, miss?

MARY. Yes, sir, I milk the cows, set up the milk, superintend the churning, and make the cheese.

ASA. Wal, darn me if you ain't the first raal right down useful gal I've seen this side of the pond.

FLORENCE. What's that, sir? Do you want to make me jealous?

ASA. Oh, no, you needn't get your back up; you are the right sort, too, but you must own you're small potatoes, and few in a hill compared to a gal like this.

FLORENCE. I'm what?

ASA. Small potatoes.

FLORE NCE. Cousin, do tell me what you mean by calling me small potatoes.

ASA. Wal, you can sing and paint, and play on the pianner, and in your own particular circle you are some pumpkins.

FLORENCE. Some pumpkins? First I am small potatoes, and now I am some pumpkins.

ASA. But she, she can milk cows, sit up butter, make cheese, and, darn me, if them ain't what I call raal downright feminine accomplishments.

FLORENCE. I do believe you are right, cousin. Mary, do allow me to congratulate you on not being small potatoes.

MARY. Well, I must look to my dairy or all my last week's milk will be spoiled. Goodbye, Florence, dear. Goodbye, Mr. Trenchard. Good morning, sir. *(Goes into the dairy cottage.)*

ASA *(following her to door)*. Good morning, miss. I'll call again.

FLORENCE. Well, cousin, what do you think of her?

ASA. Ain't she a regular snorter?

FLORENCE. A what?

ASA. Wal, perhaps I should make myself more intelligible if I said a squealer. And to think I'm keepin' that everlasting angel of a gal out of her fortune all along by this bit of paper here. *(Takes paper from pocket.)*

FLORENCE. What is that?

ASA. Old Mark Trenchard's will.

FLORENCE. I don' t want to look at it; the fortune should have come to Mary. She is the only relation in the direct line.

ASA. Say, cousin, you've not told her that darned property was left to me, have you?

FLORENCE. Do you think I had the heart to tell her of her misfortune?

ASA. Wal, darn me, if you didn't show your good sense, at any rate. *(Looks in the dairy door.)*

FLORENCE. Well, what are you doing, showing your good sense?

ASA. Oh, you go 'long. Didn't I see you casting sheep's eyes at that sailor man this morning? Say, has he got that ship yet?

FLORENCE. No, he hasn't, though I've used all my powers of persuasion with that Lord Dundreary. His father has so much influence with the Admiralty.

ASA. Wal, didn't he drop like a smoked 'possum?

FLORENCE. There you go, more American. No, he said he was very sorry, but he couldn' t.

ASA *(taking out bottle)*. Oh, he did, did he? Wal, I guess he'll do his best all the same.

FLORENCE. I shall be missed at the archery grounds. Will you take me back?

ASA. Like a streak of lightning. *(Offers arm and takes her to dairy.)*

FLORENCE. That's not the way.

ASA. No, of course not. *(Takes her around stage and back to dairy.)*

FLORENCE. Well, but where are you going now?

ASA. Say, cousin, don't you think you could find your way back alone? I want to see, to see—

FLORENCE. Why, what do you want to see?

ASA. Wal, I just wanted to see how they make cheese over here. *(Exits into the dairy.)*

FLORENCE. *(laughing).* And they call that man a savage? Well, I only wish we had a few more such savages in England. *(Executes a deep bow as the lights dim.)*

(The lights come up on the NIGHTWATCHMAN, who re-emerges from the shadows, still carrying his lantern. As he speaks, he moves in and out among the actors as they silently stand in frozen groupings.)

NIGHTWATCH MAN. Yes, this was a busy place during rehearsals, all right. Particularly that day, they tell me. For right in the middle of the morning—about 10:30 it was—a special messenger came to the theater.

(The messenger, a Private in the Union Army, enters, pantomines a conversation with the PROMPTER.)

NIGHTWATCHMAN. He went first to young Mr. Ford who was acting as manager while his father was out of town. Mr. John Ford, it was. He sent him inside to Miss Keene.

(The stage is fully lighted again. The NIGHTWATCHMAN disappears. The PROMPTER takes the SOLDIER over to LAURA KEENE.)

SOLDIER. I have been sent here, Miss Keene, to inform you that the President will require the State Box for the performance of "Our American Cousin," your esteemed success, this evening. Among his guests will be General Grant. *(The company reacts enthusiastically to this announcement.)*

LAURA KEENE. My company and I are honored Private, as I'm certain Mr. Ford is, to have the President and his party as our guests. We will decorate the State Box this afternoon in special honor of the occasion. I hope you will carry back these words to the White House.

SOLDIER. Gladly, Miss Keene.

LAURA KEENE. Thank you very much.

SOLDIER. Good morning, ma'am. *(Withdraws.)*

LAURA KEENE. Good morning, Private.

PROMPTER. Now there will be a crowd for certain.

LAURA KEENE. And we'll be ready for them. Rehearsals of the next scenes will follow as soon as proper preparations have been put in order … *(She is drowned out by the great excitement of the actors' reactions to the soldier's message. As the lights dim, the actors go off in various directions. Finally, only PEANUTS JOHN remains, standing puzzled.)*

PEANUTS JOHN *(scratching his head)*. Wonder why they're coming here instead of going over to Grover's. They got fireworks over to Grover's. *(Wanders toward the door.)* Old Abe'd like that. *(The lights dim.)*

CURTAIN

ACT II

AT RISE: *The NIGHTWATCHMAN emerges out of darkness, and crosses the stage, still swinging the lantern.*

NIGHTWATCHMAN. All evening folks lined up out front there—the way you come in just now—to get their tickets. You see, young Mr. Ford printed handbills announcing the President's attendance, and they was passed out along E Street, and up on F and G. So, it didn't take long to fill up the house. *(Sounds of the assembling audience are heard.)* And I expect as much excitement was going on behind the stage as out there, what with Miss Keene checking to see if everybody was ready …

(The lights come up on the gathering actors, all in costume now, as LAURA KEENE calls out.)

LAURA KEENE. Miss Augusta, may I see you? *(AUGUSTA comes to her, and she examines her costume closely.)* You took care of the hem, I see. Very good. You look lovely, my dear.

AUGUSTA. Thank you, Miss Keene.

LAURA KEENE. Now calm yourself until we begin.

AUGUSTA. Yes, ma'am. *(Withdraws.)*

LAURA KEENE. Mr. Buddicombe, your tie is loose again.

BUDDICOMBE *(as he comes to her)*. Miss Keene, I need a dresser. I've had one in my previous engagements—always.

LAURA KEENE. You're in my employment now. *(As she ties his tie.)* If you can't dress yourself, I will. *(Actors laugh at this.)*

BUDDICOMBE. Thank you, Miss Keene, but that won't be necessary, I assure you. *(Checks his costume in detail.)*

LAURA KEENE. Oh, Mr. Prompter, I am more worried

about you than anyone else. If you had played Harry Vernon just once before …

PROMPTER. I gave my lines exactly in today's rehearsals, Miss Keene.

LAURA KEENE. This is what we'll do: When I am offstage I'll come straight to your table, and we'll go over our scenes together. Just as a reminder.

PROMPTER. I'm certain I know them perfectly, Miss Keene.

(MR. EMERSON enters at this point.)

LAURA KEENE *(seeing him enter).* Oh, yes, Mr. Emerson. *(Gets his attention and hops. He returns the hop, smiles, and bows. She returns the bow.)* Excellent.

(PEANUTS JOHN runs in, and crosses to LAURA KEENE.)

PEANUTS JOHN. The carriages are lining up Tenth Street. And people gathering, too, just watching.

LAURA KEENE. Has the White House carriage been sighted?

PEANUTS JOHN. No, ma'am. Some say he ain't coming— that it was a trick to get folks away from Grover's. I heard 'em say that, Miss Keene. They say you tricked them, and they don't like it.

LAURA KEENE. Young man, you tell them to come into the play, and see if they don't like that. *(Turns away.)* Now, Mrs. Mountchessington, I meant to ask you this morning about your laugh. I fear it's becoming somewhat obtrusive. *(As she pantomimes a conversation with MRS. MOUNTCHESSINGTON, the lights fade back to the NIGHTWATCHMAN. All of the actors stand frozen their positions as he speaks.)*

NIGHTWATCHMAN. They come in, they did, all the way to the last rows of the galleries—and all of them in a holiday spirit. And even though the President's party hadn't arrived, Miss Keene started the play on time, and the audience began to laugh. *(Disappears. Laughter is heard in the darkness.)*

(Slowly the lights come up on the actors in their places for the following scene which is played exactly as it was in Act I. They begin the scene in darkness.)

FLORENCE. Then recollect that you have an appointment with me after luncheon.

DUNDREARY. Yeth, yeth.

FLORENCE. Well, what have you after luncheon?

DUNDREARY. Well, sometimes I have a glass of brandy with an egg in it, sometimes a run around the duck pond, sometimes a game of checkers—that's for exercise—and sometimes a game of billiards. *(Audience laughter is heard.)*

FLORENCE. No, no! You have with me after luncheon, an ap—an ap—

DUNDREARY. An ap—an ap—

FLORE NCE. An ap—an appoint—appointment.

DUNDREARY. An ointment, that's the idea. *(Laughter from audience. The lights fade as the actors hold their positions. The NIGHTWATCHMAN appears and moves among the frozen actors toward the Presidential box.)*

NIGHTWATCHMAN. Just at 8:25 the Presidential party arrived. They came up the stairs and around the hall to the entrance of the box. *(Moves into the box.)* The President came to the front of the box. And bowed. They tell me everybody in the house stood up. *(The actors on the stage bow to the NIGHTWATCHMAN standing in the front of the box.)* The orchestra played and the crowd cheered. *(Music of "Hail to the Chief" strikes up in the background.)* Then he took his chair, just about here, I calculate. Seated over there was Major Rathbone and his pretty fiancee, Miss Clara Harris. They was the Lincolns' guests when General Grant learned he had to go on North that night and not stay in Washington. Back here to the side was Mrs. Lincoln. *(After the actors have bowed, the music stops, and they resume the play.)*

DUNDREARY. You see, I gave her a draught that cured the effect of the draught, and that draught was a draught that didn't pay the doctor's bill.

FLORENCE. But, sir, the draft has been suspended.

DUNDREARY. I don't see the joke.

FLORENCE. Why, sir, anybody can see that. *(Bows in the direction of the box. There is general laughter as the lights go down. The actors assume positions for the scene that follows.)*

NIGHTWATCHMAN. All went well—every laugh came loud and clear—the actors gave their best performances.

(He looks toward the stage and is swallowed in darkness as DUNDREARY and GEORGINA enter.)

DUNDREARY. Now, let me administer to your wants. Allow me to lead you to a seat.

GEORGINA. No, my lord, I'm too delicate. *(Sits on a three legged stool and nearly falls off.)*

DUNDREARY. Won't you take a little refreshment: a strawberry, perhaps?

GEORGINA. No, thank you.

DUNDREARY. Could you master a peanut? There is a great deal of nourishment in a peanut.

GEORGINA. No, I'm so delicate.

DUNDREARY. Then what can I do for you?

GEORGINA. If you please, ask the dairy maid to let me have a seat in the dairy. I am afraid of the draft here.

DUNDREARY. Oh! you want to get out of the draft, do you? Well, you're not the only one that wants to escape the draft. *(Bows to the presidential box as the audience applauds.)* Is that the dairy on top of that pole?

GEORGINA. No, my lord, that's the pigeon house.

DUNDREARY. What do they keep in pigeon houses? Oh! Pigeons, to be sure. They couldn't keep donkeys up there, could they? What do they keep in dairies?

GEORGINA. Eggs, milk, butter and cheese.

DUNDREARY. What's the name of that animal with a head on it? No, I don't mean that, all animals have heads. I mean those animals with something growing out of their heads.

GEORGINA. A cow?

DUNDREARY. A cow growing out of his head?

GEORGINA. No, no, horns.

DUNDREARY. A cow! Well, that accounts for the milk and butter; but I don't see the eggs; cows don't give eggs, do they? Then there's the cheese—do you like cheese?

GEORGINA. No, my lord.

DUNDREARY. Does your brother like cheese?

GEORGINA. I have no brother. I'm so delicate.

DUNDREARY. She's so delicate, she hasn't got a brother. Well, if you had a brother, do you think he'd like cheese?

GEORGINA. I don't know; do please take me to the dairy.

DUNDREARY. Well, I shall see if I can get you a broiled sardine. *(Exits into the dairy.)*

GEORGINA *(jumping up as soon as he is off)*. Oh! I'm so glad he's gone. I am dreadful hungry. I should like a plate of corn beef and cabbage, eggs and bacon, and a slice of cold ham and pickles.

DUNDREARY *(offstage)*. Thank you, thank you.

GEORGINA *(running back to seat)*. Here he comes. Oh! I'm so delicate.

(DUNDREARY enters.)

DUNDREARY. I beg your pardon, Miss Georgina, but I find upon inquiry that cows don't give sardines. But I've arranged it with the dairy maid so that you can have a seat by the window that overlooks the cow house and the pig sty, and all the pretty things.

(They go to the dairy door; GEORGINA goes in. ASA enters with two milk pails on a yoke, and watches DUNDREARY.)

DUNDREARY. That lovely Georgina puts me in mind of that beautiful piece of poetry. Let me see how it goes. The rose is red, the violet's blue—The rose is red, the violet's blue, sugar is sweet, and so is somebody, and so is somebody else. *(ASA comes up behind him and puts yoke on DUNDREARY's shoulders gently. DUNDREARY looks at the milk pails.)* I wonder what the devil this is? *(Lowers one pail, then the other; they trip him.)* Oh, I see, somebody has been fishing and caught a pail. *(Goes hopping up stage, stumbling against spinning wheel.)*

ASA. Say, whiskers, I want to ask a favor of you.

DUNDREARY *(attempting to sneeze)*. Now I've got it.

ASA *(taking his hand)*. How are you?

DUNDREARY. There, you've spoiled it.

ASA. Spoiled what?

DUNDREARY. "Spoiled what?" Why, a magnificent sneeze!

ASA. Oh? Was that what you was trying to get through you?

DUNDREARY. Get through me? He's mad.

ASA. Say, do you know Lieutenant Vernon?

DUNDREARY. Slightly.

ASA. Wal, what do you think of him, on an average?

DUNDREARY. Think of a man on an average?

ASA. Wal, I think he's a real hoss, and he wants a ship.

DUNDREARY. Well, if he's a real boss, he must want a carriage.

ASA. Darn me, if that ain't good. *(Laughs.)*

DUNDREARY. That's good. *(Laughs vigorously.)*

ASA. Yes, that is good.

DUNDREARY. Very good.

ASA. Very good indeed, for you. I want your influence, sir, to get that ship.

DUNDREARY. I want all my influence, sir, for my own w—w—welations.

ASA *(mimicking)*. Oh, you want it for your own w—w—welations.

DUNDREARY. I say, sir, you stutter. I'll give you a k—k—k—

ASA. No, you won't give me a kick.

DUNDREARY. I'll give you a c—c—card to a doctor and he'll c—c—

ASA. No, he won't kick me, either.

DUNDREARY. He's idiotic. I don't mean that. He'll cure you.

ASA. Same one that cured you?

DUNDREARY. The same.

ASA. Wal, if you're cured, I want to stay sick. Darn me, look at your whiskers.

DUNDREARY. My whiskers!

ASA. Yes, about the ends they're black, and near the roots they're all speckled.

DUNDREARY *(horror struck)*. My whiskers speckled and streaked?

ASA *(showing bottle)*. Now, this is a wonderful invention.

DUNDREARY. My hair dye. My dear sir.

ASA *(squeezing his hand)*. How are you?

DUNDREARY. Dear Mr. Trenchard.

ASA. Now, look here. You get the lieutenant a ship and I'll give you the bottle. It's a fine swap.

DUNDREARY. What the devil is a swap?

ASA. Well, you give me a ship and I'll give you the bottle to boot.

DUNDREARY. What do I want of your boots?

ASA. You'd better make haste, or your whiskers will be a pea green in about a minute.

DUNDREARY. Pea green! *(Exits hastily.)*

ASA. I guess I've got a ring in his nose now. I wonder how that sick gal is getting along. *(Looks into dairy.)* Wal, darn me, if the dying swallow ain't pitching into ham and eggs and home-made bread. I'll just give her a start. How de do, miss! Allow me to congratulate you on the return of your appetite. *(GEORGINA screams.)* Guess I've got a ring in her pretty nose now. *(Looks off.)* Hello! Here comes the shooters.

(SIR EDWARD, MRS. MOUNTCHESSINGTON, FLOR-ENCE, AUGUSTA, WICKENS, COYLE, BINNY, SKILLET and BUDDICOMBE enter. BUDDICOMBE is carrying tray and glasses.)

SIR EDWARD. Now to distribute the prizes, and to drink to the health of the winner of the golden arrow.

FLORENCE. And there stands the hero of the day. Come, kneel down.

ASA. Must I kneel down?

FLORENCE. I am going to crown you Captain of the Archers of Trenchard Manor.

ASA *(whispering to FLORENCE)*. I've got the ship.

FLORENCE. No, have you?

SIR EDWARD. Come, ladies and gentlemen, take from me. *(Offers drinks.)* Who are those strange faces approaching?

COYLE *(in his ear)*. Bailiffs, Sir Edward.

SIR EDWARD. Bailiffs! Florence, I am lost! *(FLORENCE supports her father. ASA opens a bottle that pops, causing everyone to run offstage in distress and confusion as the lights dim out. The sound of applause is heard as the actors and stagehands move the scenery quickly and quietly. The orchestra plays; the scene is set and ready.)*

PROMPTER *(whispering to an actor).* Have the gas man bring up the front gas. Dairy lights ready? Begin. *(The lights fade to the dairy scene.)*

ASA. Miss Mary, I wish you'd leave off those dairy fixings, and take a hand of chat along with me.

MARY. Law, Mr. Trenchard, what a strange man you are! First you were so bashful you would hardly speak; now you are here every day.

ASA. I've got a heap to say to you, and I never can talk while you're moving about so spry among them pans, pails, and cheeses. It takes the gumption right out of me.

MARY. Well, then, I'll sit here. *(Sits on bench with ASA, vis-a-vis.)* Well, now, will that do?

ASA. Well, no, Miss Mary, that won't do, neither. Them eyes of yourn takes my breath away.

MARY. What will do, then?

ASA. Well, I don' t know, Miss Mary. But, darn me, if you could do anything that wasn't so 'tarnal neat and handsome, that a fellow would want you to keep on doing nothing else all the time.

MARY. Well, then, I'll go away. *(Rises.)*

ASA *(stopping her).* No, don't do that, Miss Mary. *(Sits.)* Somehow I feel kinder lost, if I haven't got you to talk to. Now that I've got the latitude and longitude of all them big folks at the Manor House, found out the length of every lady's foot, and the soft spot on everybody's head, they can't teach me nothing. But here, here I come to school. *(Whittles.)*

MARY. Then throw away that stick, and put away your knife, like a good boy. *(He throws away stick.)* I must cure you of that dreadful trick of whittling.

ASA. Oh, if you only knew how it helps me to keep my eyes off you, Miss Mary.

MARY. But you needn't keep your eyes off me.

ASA. I'm afraid I must. My eyes are awful tale-tellers, and they might be saying something you wouldn't like to hear. That might make you mad, and then you'd shut up school, and send me home feeling about as small as a tadpole with his tail bobbed off.

MARY. Don't be alarmed. I don't think I will listen to any tales that your eyes may tell, unless they're tales I like and ought to hear.

ASA. If I thought they'd tell any others, Miss Mary, I'd pluck them right out and throw them in the first turnip patch I came to.

MARY. And now tell me more about your home in America. I can shut my eyes and almost fancy I see your home in the backwoods. *(Does so.)* There's your mother, seated near the fire, and you and your brothers come in all covered with snow. And your two sisters running about in their sunbonnets.

ASA. Debby and Nab? Yes!

MARY. Then there's doughnuts and corn cakes and a demi-john of peach brandy.

ASA. I shall faint in about five minutes.

MARY. Then how we lasses bustle about to prepare supper. The fire blazes on the hearth, while your good old mother cooks the slapjacks. Do you know, Mr. Trenchard, you have made me half a backwoodsman's wife already?

ASA. I wish I could make you a whole one. I say, Miss Mary, you ought to make tracks.

MARY. Make what?

ASA. Pack up, and emigrate to the roaring old state of Vermont, and live 'long with mother. She'd make you so comfortable. And there would be sister Debby and Nab, and well, I reckon I'd be there, too.

MARY. Oh! I'm afraid if I were there your mother would find the poor English girl a sad encumbrance.

ASA. Oh, she ain't proud, not a mite; besides, they've all seen Britishers before.

MARY. I suppose you allude to my cousin, Edward Trenchard?

ASA. Wal, he ain't the only one. There was the old squire, Mark Trenchard.

MARY. My grandfather!

ASA. Oh! he was a fine old hoss. You see, he was kinder mad with his folks here, so he came over to America to look after the original branch of the family. That's our branch.

MARY. Tell me, Mr. Trenchard, did he ever receive any letters from his daughter?

ASA. Oh, yes, lots of them. But the old cuss chucked them in the fire as soon as he made out who they come from.

MARY. My poor mother.

ASA. You see, as nigh as we could reckon it up, she'd gone and got married against his will, and that made him mad. Well, he was a queer kind of rusty, fusty, old coon, and it appeared that he got older, and rustier, and fustier, and fustier, and coonier every fall. You see, it always took him in the fall. He got took down with the ague. He was so bad the doctors gave him up, and mother, she went for a minister. While she was gone the old man called me in his room. "Come in, Asa, boy," says he, and his voice rang loud and clear as a bell. "Sit down," says he. You see, I was always a favorite with the old man. "Asa, my boy," says he, takin' a great piece of paper, "when I die, this sheet of paper makes you heir to all my property in England." The old Squire was sitting up in his bed, his face as pale as the sheet that covered him, his silken hair flowing in silvery locks from under his red cap, and the tears rolling from his large blue eyes down his furrowed cheeks, like two millstreams. *(Breaking.)* Will you excuse my lighting a cigar? For the story is awful long and I don't think I can get through it without a smoke. *(Strikes match.)* Three days passed and he called me in again. "Wal," says he to me, and his voice was not as loud as it was afore-it was like the whisper of the wind in a pine forest, low and awful. "Asa, boy," says he, "I feel that I've sinned in hardening my heart against my own flesh and blood. Give me the light," says he. Wal, I gave him the candle that stood by his bedside, and he took the sheet of paper. Just as I might take this. *(Takes will from pocket.)* And he twisted it up as I might this. *(Lights will.)* And he lights it just this way. And he watched it burn slowly and slowly away. Then, says he, "Asa, boy, that act disi nherits you, but it leaves all my property to one who has a better right to it. My own daughter's darling child, Mary Meredith." Do you object to smoke?

MARY. Poor grandfather. *(Buries her face and sobs.)*

ASA. Wal, I guess I'd better let her be. *(Sees half-burned will.)* There's four hundred thousand dollars, up in smoke. Asa, boy, you're a boss, by thunder. *(Exits.)*

MARY *(looking up)*. Oh, Mr. Trenchard, how we have all wronged poor grandfather. What, gone? He felt after such tidings I should be left alone. Who would suspect there was such delicacy under that rough husk? But I can hardly believe the startling news. I, the penniless orphan of an hour ago, no longer penniless? But, alas, still an orphan, with none to share my wealth, none to love me.

(Enter FLORENCE.)

FLORENCE *(throwing her arms around MARY's neck)*. Mary, no one to love you, eh? What's the matter? I met that American grizzly bear coming from here. He has not been rude to you?

MARY. Oh, no, he's the gentlest of human beings. But he has just told me that all grandfather's property is mine. Mine, Florence. Do you understand?

FLORENCE. Why, you know Mark Trenchard left everything to Asa. Did he ask you to marry him?

MARY. No, no, you have been misinformed.

FLORENCE. Nonsense, he showed me the will not an hour ago on a half sheet of rough paper, just like this. *(Sees will.)* Like this. *(Picks it up.)* Why, this is part of it, I believe.

MARY. That's the paper he lighted his cigar with.

FLORENCE. Then that noble fellow lit his cigar with his fortune that you might have it. Here are the words: "Asa Trenchard, in consideration of sole heir—"

MARY. Oh, Florence, what does this mean?

FLORENCE. It means that he is a true hero, and he loves you, you little rogue. *(Embraces her.)*

MARY. Generous man.

FLORENCE. Let's find him out at once!

(They run off as MRS. MOUNTCHESSINGTON and AUGUSTA enter.)

MRS. MOUNTCH ESSINGTON. Now, Augusta, I wish you to be very attentive to Mr. Trenchard, my dear.

AUGUSTA *(bored)*. What would you advise, Ma? You know I am always advised by you.

MRS. MOUNTCHESSINGTON. Just remember, dear, he's rich, that's all. Hush, here he comes.

(Enter ASA.)

MRS. MOUNTCHESSINGTON. Ah, Mr. Trenchard! We were just saying how you always seem sure of hitting your mark—the gold ring, I mean.

ASA. Why, it's very easy, you see. I guess it's like most things in life. You fix your eyes upon the target, look straight, pull strong, calculate the distance, and twang, you're sure to hit the mark.

MRS. MOUNTCHESSINGTON. Oh, Mr. Trenchard, you are so clever.

AUGUSTA. Yes, so clever.

ASA. Thank you, Miss 'Gusty.

MRS. MOUNTCHESSINGTON *(carried away)*. So clever, so eccentric, and so rich! But what are riches compared to affection? People sometimes look a great way off, for that which is near at hand. *(Glances at AUGUSTA and ASA alternately.)*

ASA. You don't mean Miss 'Gusty here. *(Winks sheepishly at AUGUSTA.)*

AUGUSTA. He did it, Ma. He did it again.

ASA *(to himself)*. This old gal is trying to get me on a string. *(Aloud.)* Wal, it's nice to know that if a homespun feller like me was to come forward as a suitor for Miss 'Gusty's hand, you wouldn't treat me as some folks do when they find out I wasn't heir to the fortune.

MRS. MOUNTCHESSINGTON. You're joking!

AUGUSTA. Yes, you are joking. *(Forces a loud laugh.)*

ASA. No, he thought better on leaving it to me, and made his sole heir Miss Mary Meredith.

MRS. MOUNTCHESSINGTON *(shocked)*. Miss Mary Meredith! Oh, I'm delighted.

AUGUSTA. Delighted?

ASA. Yes, you both look tickled to death, you do. So you see I've no money but I'm boiling over with love and affection, and ready to pour it out like apple sass over roast pork.

MRS. MOUNTCHESSINGTON. Mr. Trenchard, please remember you are addressing my daughter, in my presence.

ASA. Yes, I'm offering my hand—with nothing in it.

MRS. MOUNTCHESSINGTON. Augusta, dear, to your room.

AUGUSTA. Yes, Ma. The nasty beast. *(Exits.)*

MRS. MOUNTCHESSINGTON. Sir, your vulgarity renders you intolerable in polite society! *(Exits.)*

ASA. Maybe I don't know the manners of polite society. But I guess I know enough to turn you inside out, old gal—you sockdologizing old mantrap.

(The sound of a shot is heard. The lights rapidly fade and come up on the NIGHTWATCHMAN, standing in the presidential box.)

NIGHTWATCHMAN. Only Asa Trenchard was on stage at that moment. Stood just about there. *(ASA holds his position.)* And that's when it happened. John Wilkes Booth came into the box here, and fired the derringer. He jumped over the side, down to the stage. But he caught his spur in the flag draped on the box and hit up against the picture of George Washington. He fell, hurt himself, and some say, shouted, "*Sic semper tyrannis*," as he hobbled out through the stage door where his horse was waiting. *(ASA withdraws. The stage is empty except for the NIGHTWATCHMAN.)* Mr. Lincoln slumped in his chair. Mrs. Lincoln got to her feet and cried for help. They carried him across the street to the Peterson House. And you know the rest, I suppose? He died the next morning; about six o' clock, it was. Mr. Ford was arrested. The Government seized the theatre; had to pay dearly for it, too. $100,000 it cost them. Then they didn't know what to do with it. Finally they put floors in and made government offices. And now the worst calamity of all, the worst in the Capital's history. The floors up there giving in, killing all those innocent people. You see why I said it's like a tomb here. *(Crosses the stage.)* It's a strange story, all right. Some say that shot was heard 'round the world. And I know it sure enough changed the history of this country. There was folks who couldn't get over it. Major Rathbone married that pretty Miss Harris, and one morning went mad and murdered her. Spent the rest of his days in the asylum. Mrs. Lincoln, too, was finally declared a lunatic and committed. *(Pause.)* No, the actors never got to finish their play that night. They moved on like actors do. But do you know for a fact that when I'm here at night, sometimes I get a feeling they've come back? Now I don't believe in ghosts, mind you, and I ain't saying I ever saw them, not one of them. But every once in a while the light from the street falls on the floor like a stage light, and voices from outside echo in here and seem to stay. When that happens I always think they're here finishing their play.

(It happens. The lights fade as the actors resume their positions. The NIGHTWATCHMAN wanders out among them and disappears. Enter ASA, followed by MARY.)

MARY. Why, Mr. Trenchard, what have you done?

ASA. Nothing but my duty, Mary.

MARY. What can I say but to offer you my lifelong gratitude—

ASA. Don't, now, miss, don't—

MARY. If I knew what else to offer …

ASA. Why, give me yourself, Mary. Oh, I know what a rude, ill-mannered block I am. But there is a heart inside me worth something, if it's only your dear little image that's planted right plump in thr middle of it.

MARY. If you think the love of one as humble as myself is worth accepting, I am yours.

ASA. You are? *(Seizes her hand suddenly; then drops it.)* Hold on, now. If this is a sacrifice you are making out of gratitude to me, I'll not have it. Though not having it will nigh break my heart, as tough as it is.

MARY. No, no, I give myself freely to you—as freely as you, this morning, gave my grandfather's property to me. I call upon my mother's gentle spirit to witness: I'll be to you a true and loving wife.

ASA *(clasping her in his arms)*. Mary, you' ll not repent it. I'm rough, Mary, awful rough. But you needn't fear that I'll ever be rough to you. I've camped out in the woods, Mary, and seen the bears at play with their cubs in the moonlight, the glistening teeth that would tear the hunter were harmless to them. The strong claws that would peel a man's head as a knife would a pumpkin was as soft for them as velvet cushions. That's what. I'll be with you, my own little wife. If ever harm does come to you, Mary, it must come over the dead body of Asa Trenchard. Wal, if I don't get out in the air, I'll bust. *(Exits hastily, pulling MARY after him.)*

(MR. BINNY runs on, a little drunk.)

MR. BINNY *(calling)*. Mr. H'asa. Mr H'asa? Oh, he's gone. I suppose he'll come back to keep his appointment in the wine cellar. It isn't h'often that h'an H'american has the run of the wine cellars of Trenchard Manor, and in such company, too. There's me and Mr. Coyle, a good judge of old port wine, his clerk, Mr. Murcott, which I don't h'exactly like sitting down with clerks. But he is a man of h'edication, though unfortunately taken to drink. *(Hiccups.)* Well, that's been many a man's misfortune, though I say it, what shouldn't say it, being a butler. *(Hiccups again.)*

(The lights shift to the wine cellar, lighted only by candles. COYLE and MURCOTT take seats at the table, both well intoxicated.)

MR. COYLE. A capital glass of wine, capital. *(ASA calls from without.)*

ASA *(offstage)*. Bring a light here, can't you? I've broken my natural allowances of shins already.

(ASA enters.)

ASA *(to MR. MURCOTT)*. Is he tight yet?

MR. MURCOTT. Not quite gone yet.

MR. COYL E. Oh, Mr. Trenchard, glad to see you. Welcome to the vaults of your ancestors.

ASA. Wal, you seem to be punishing their spirits pretty well.

(MR. BINNY stumbles in.)

MR. BINNY. Wines, Mr. Asa. The spirits are in the h'outer cellar.

ASA *(to COYLE, who is singing)*. Sh! Softly!

MR. COYL E. Here you might bawl yourself hoarse beneath these ribs of stone, and nobody hear you. *(Sings louder.)*

MR. BINNY. Sing h'as loud h'as you like. *(Falls over a barrel and then into it.)*

ASA. Steady, old hoss, steady.

MR. BINNY. I'm h'always steady. *(Goes to sleep, sitting in barrel, legs hanging over side.)*

MR. COYLE *(singing)*. "We won't go home until morning. Oh, we won't go home until morning."

ASA *(singing)*. "I don't think you'll go home at all!" Now then, quick, Murcott, get the keys to his case here. *(MURCOTT gets keys from COYLE's pocket, throws them to ASA.)* Is this all?

MR. MURCOTT *(trembling)*. The key to his private case is on his watch chain. I can't get it off.

ASA. Take watch and all.

MR. MURCOTT. He will accuse me of robbing him.

ASA. Never mind. I'll take the responsibility. *(COYLE moves.)*

MR. MURCOTT. He is getting up.

ASA. Wal, darn me, knock him down.

MR. MURCOTT. I can't.

ASA. Can't you? Wal, darn me, I can. *(Slightly tips COYLE, who falls back into the chair.)* Have you found it?

MR. MURCOTT *(trembling)*. I'm too weak. Too weak!

ASA. I'll open it myself. I'm the best key they ever invented.

MR. MURCOTT. Oh, my poor muddled brain, what does he mean? Key, what key?

ASA. What key? Why, Yankee! *(Pulls open the case as COYLE sits up.)*

MR. COYLE. Villains! Would you rob me?

MR. MURCOTT. Stand off, Coyle, we are desperate.

ASA *(taking out paper)*. Here it is, as sure as there are snakes in old Virginia. Let the old cuss go, Murcott.

MR. COYLE. Oh, you shall pay dearly for this. The law shall aid me.

ASA. It might look further than I calculate is convenient for you.

MR. COYLE. So, gentlemen, I am in your power. How much do you want?

ASA. You have an appointment with Sir Edward, haven't you? Wal, I want you to keep it! Instead of saying you have come to foreclose the mortgage, I want you to say you have found the release which proves the mortgage has been paid off.

MR. COYLE. Is that all?

ASA. Not half. Next, apologize to Miss Florence for having had the impudence to ask her hand in marriage.

MR. COYLE. What then?

ASA. Then give up your agency of Sir Edward's estates to your clerk, Abel Murcott.

MR. COYLE. What, he, the drunkard?

ASA. He that was, but he that's going to take the pledge at the first pump he comes to.

MR. MURCOTT. Yes, I will conquer demon drink. Or die in the struggle.

MR. COYL E. Is that all?

ASA. No, you better wash your face. You're not the best-looking man when you're clean, and now you're awful. *(COYLE makes a dash at MURCOTT, who trips him, and leads him out.)* Mr. Coyle, you will have the first wash. To the pump, Murcott.

MR. MURCOTT. Give me strength! Courage! Courage! Courage!

(They go off and the lights shift to the Dairy scene which follows immediately. LORD DUNDREARY enters, followed by HARRY VERNON. As usual, DUNDREARY is about to sneeze.)

VERNON. My lord! Your lordship. *(Puts his hand on DUN-DREARY's arm.)* My lord, I only wanted to …

DUNDREARY. There you go. Now you've spoiled it!

VERNON. Spoiled what, my lord?

DUNDREARY. Spoiled what? Why, a most magnificent sneeze.

VERNON. I'm very sorry to interrupt, but I merely wanted to express my gratitude to you for getting me a ship.

DUNDREARY. I don't want your gratitude; I want to sneeze.

VERNON. Very well, my lord, I will leave you, and thus give the opportunity for sneezing. But if Harry Vernon can ever be of any service to you, give him a call, and he'll be alongside. *(Salutes and exits.)*

DUNDREARY. What does he mean, a long side? Is one side longer than another? What's the matter with the sailor's side? Oh, I see. He's got the stomachache. That's the idea. *(Exits.)*

(A clock strikes two. SIR EDWARD enters.)

SIR EDWARD. The clock is on the stroke of two, and Coyle is waiting my decision. No, no, I will not sacrifice her young life so full of promise. Better to leave her to the mercy of chance than sell her to this scoundrel. I will not survive the downfall of my house, but end my woes at once. *(Puts pistol to his head.)*

(FLORENCE rushes in and stops him.)

FLORENCE. Dear Father, I know all, and will consent to marry this man although I shall die at the altar.

(ASA, COYLE and MURCOTI enter.)

ASA. This way, Mr. Coyle.

SIR EDWARD. How is this, Mr. Coyle? You are not alone?

ASA. Wal, you see, Squire, Mr. Coyle here wishes me and his clerk to witness cutting off the seals from the mortgage, which he has been lucky enough to find the release on.

SIR EDWARD. Heavens, is it so?

MR. COYLE. Yes, Sir Edward, there is the release executed by my father, which had become detached.

ASA *(whispering to COYLE)*. Accidentally.

MR. COYL E. Accidentally.

SIR EDWARD. But my daughter, sir?

MR. COYLE. I regret that I should have conceived so mad a

thought. It is enough to unfit me for longer holding position as your agent, which I beg humbly to resign.

ASA *(prompting him)*. Recommending as my successor—

MR. COYLE. Recommending as my successor, Abel Murcott, whose knowledge of your affairs will render him as useful as I have been.

ASA. And now, my dear Mr. Coyle, you may a-b-s-q-u-a-t-u-l-a-t-e.

MR. COYLE. I go, Sir Edward, with equal good wishes for all assembled here. *(As he exits, he leers at ASA and MURCOTT.)*

ASA. That's a good man, Sir Edward.

SIR EDWARD. Yes, he's a good man.

ASA. But he can't keep a hotel.

SIR EDWARD. Now, Mr. Murcott, your offense was great, but your punishment has been greater.

FLORENCE. Mr. Murcott, my father forgives you although he does not yet know all you have done for us. I thank you, Mr. Murcott, for you have saved me.

MR. MURCOTT *(taking her hand and kissing it)*. Thank heaven, thank heaven! I have saved her. I am good for something at last. *(Exits.)*

FLORENCE. You'll keep your promise and make Mr. Murcott your clerk, Father?

SIR EDWARD. I can refuse nothing today, I am so happy.

(VERNON enters and joins FLORENCE.)

ASA. Can't you, Sir Edward? Now, that's awfully lucky, for there's two gals want your consent mighty bad.

SIR EDWARD. Indeed, sir, for what?

ASA. To get hitched.

SIR EDWARD. Hitched?

ASA. Yes, to get spliced.

SIR EDWARD. Spliced?

ASA. Yes, to get married.

SIR EDWARD. Who are they?

ASA *(pointing to FLORENCE)*. There's one of them, and the other is right outside. *(Rushes out.)*

SIR EDWARD. You have my consent, Florence. Vernon, take her; she's yours. Though Heaven knows what I shall do without her.

FLORENCE. Thank you, Father, for this day, the happiest of my life.

VERNON. Thank you, Sir Edward. I shall always make Miss Florence the happiest sailor's wife in the world. *(Salutes.)*

(ASA re-enters with MARY.)

ASA. Here's the other one, Sir Edward.

SIR EDWARD. Mary, whom have you chosen?

MARY. Rough-spun, honest-hearted Asa Trenchard.

SIR EDWARD. Then, Mr. Trenchard, you win a heart of gold.

FLORENCE. And so does Mary, Papa, believe me. *(To ASA.)* Why, what's the matter, Mr. Trenchard?

ASA. You make me blush all the way down my back. Wal, looka here, here comes the whole household looking awful romantic. Here's Mrs. Mountchessington. Here's Miss 'Gusty, who didn't get a man.

(MRS. MOUNTCHESSINGTON and AUGUSTA enter as ASA calls off their names.)

MRS. MOUNTCHESSINGTON. I beg your pardon, but she did. Captain de Boots is sending a horse for her this very minute.

ASA. Now, Miss 'Gusty, you're a regular hoss for certain, like I always said.

AUGUSTA. I'm not going to marry the horse, but Captain de Boots!

ASA. And dang me if here ain't old sneeze-it and the sick girl.

(DUNDREARY and GEORGINA enter.)

DUNDREARY. There's that darned rhinoceros again. *(Seats GEORGINA.)*

ASA. And here's Puffy and his gal.

(MR. BINNY and SKILLET enter and bow.)

FLORENCE. Then we're all getting married.

DUNDREARY. Yes, it's contagious, like the cholera.

MR. BINNY. I 'ope, Sir H'edward, there h'are no objections to my leading Miss Skillet to the 'ymeneal h'altar.

SIR EDWARD. Certainly not, Mr. Binny.

SKILLET. I'm thanking you, sir, I am.

ASA *(to DUNDREARY)*. Say, Lord Button. I say, Whiskers—

DUNDREARY. Yes, illustrious exile?

ASA. They're a nice color, aren't they?

DUNDREARY. They're all wight now.

ASA. All wight? Dang me, but they're all black.

DUNDREARY. But when I say wight I mean black.

ASA. Say, shall I tell that gal about the dye stuff?

DUNDREARY. Well, I'd rather you wouldn't.

ASA. Well, I won't if you don't want me to. *(Slaps DUN-DREARY on the back warmheartedly. Then he goes to GEORGINA and sits in her lap.)* Miss Georgina, how's your appetite? Shall I tell Lord Sneeze-it about the beefsteak and onions I saw you pitching into?

GEORGINA. Please don't, Mr. Trenchard. I'm so delicate. *(Lifts him up and stands him on the floor.)*

ASA. Well, I won't if you don't want me to. *(Goes to AUGUSTA.)* Wal, Miss 'Gusty, you got your boots, have you?

AUGUSTA. Yes, Mr. Trenchard.

ASA *(whispering)*. Shall I tell him you were after me first?

AUGUSTA & MRS. MOUNTCHESSINGTON. Not for the world, Mr. Trenchard.

ASA. Well, I won't if you don't want me to. *(Goes to MR. BINNY.)* Say, Mr. Puffy, shall I tell Sir Edward about your getting drunk in the wine cellar?

MR. BINNY. You need not.

ASA. Wal, I won't if you don't want me to.

FLORENCE. Come, cousin, have you nothing to say to us?

ASA. Wal, the way I calculate it, we're all as happy as oysters at high water.

FLORENCE. I'm sure of it, thanks to you, Our American Cousin.

ASA. I'm mighty glad I come. *(Takes MARY's hand.)*

FLORENCE. But, don't go yet, pray. For Lord Dundreary has a word to say. Lord Dundreary. *(DUNDREARY builds up to a gigantic sneeze, and for the first time is not interrupted. After the loud sneeze, he beams.)*

DUNDREARY. That's the idea? *(They all laugh as the scene fades. The actors disappear into the darkness.)*

(All is quiet. Then the door opens as it did in the beginning of the play, and the NIGHTWATCHMAN appears once more. He lifts his lantern high as he crosses.)

NIGHTWATCHMAN. Did you hear something? Sounded like a sneeze to me. We'll be able to see now when the sun hits the window. *(Indicates a window offstage.)* There she is. *(A beam of light breaks through the darkness. He looks upstage.)* Why, nobody's there in those ruins. *(Turns as if speaking to someone at his side.)* I told you this place is strange, all right. *(Then looking about him.)* Why, there's nobody here, either ... *(Not able to understand, he stares in puzzlement. Then he looks up into the light.)* Oh, I'm happy to see the morning.

SLOW CURTAIN

NOTES

NOTES

NOTES

NOTES